MW01700783

Bats of Krau Wildlife Reserve

Bats of Krau Wildlife Reserve

Tigga Kingston
Lim Boo Liat
Zubaid Akbar

PENERBIT UNIVERSITI KEBANGSAAN MALAYSIA
BANGI · 2006
http://www.penerbit.ukm.my

Cetakan Pertama / *First Printing*, 2006

Diterbitkan di Malaysia oleh / *Published in Malaysia by*
PENERBIT UNIVERSITI KEBANGSAAN MALAYSIA
43600 UKM Bangi, Selangor D. E., Malaysia
http://www.penerbit.ukm.my
e-mail: penerbit@pkrisc.cc.ukm.my

Penerbit UKM adalah anggota / *is a member of the*
PERSATUAN PENERBIT BUKU MALAYSIA /
MALAYSIAN BOOK PUBLISHERS ASSOCIATION
No. Ahli / *Membership No.* 198302

Dicetak di Malaysia oleh / *Printed in Malaysia by*
AMPANG PRESS SDN. BHD.
6, Jalan 6/91, Taman Shamelin Perkasa
Batu 3½ Jalan Cheras
56100 Kuala Lumpur, MALAYSIA
E-mail: ampress@streamyx.com

Perpustakaan Negara Malaysia
Data-Pengkatalogan-dalam-Penerbitan /
Cataloguing-in-Publication Data

Kingston, Tigga
Bats of krau wildlife reserve / by Tigga Kingston, Lim Boo Liat, Zubaid Akbar.
Includes index
Bibliography: p. 141
1. Bats--Pahang--Krau. 2. Wildlife conservation--Pahang--Krau.
I. Lim, Boo Liat. II. Zubaid Akbar. I. Title.
599.409595123

ISBN 967-942-756-0

Contents

List of Figures

Preface

With at least 69 species, Krau Wildlife Reserve (KWR) in the state of Pahang, Malaysia, supports the highest diversity of bats recorded anywhere in the Old World and is consequently a critical site for global bat conservation. The bat fauna of KWR is also the best known in the region; it has been the focus of over 20 published studies in the last thirty years, and is currently the subject of intensive study by the Malaysian Bat Conservation Research Unit (MBCRU). The long history of bat research in KWR, coupled with the unique bat diversity that the reserve supports, provide the inspiration for this book. Our aim is to synthesize past and present research on the bats of KWR and to provide comprehensive accounts of each species that will be of use to future researchers both within and beyond the reserve. Few people have the chance to see bats up close, so perhaps more than anything this book is also a celebration of the extraordinary physical and ecological diversity of bats that dwell in Malaysia's incredible rainforests. We hope this book provides the reader with a small window into their world; a chance to appreciate this globally unique component of Malaysia's biodiversity heritage and the importance of Krau Wildlife Reserve in preserving it.

This book draws heavily on research conducted by the MBCRU, supported by grants to Boston University and to Tigga Kingston from the U.S. National Science Foundation (award number: DEB 0108384), Earthwatch Institute, and National Geographic Society. We thank the students of the MBCRU for contributing their knowledge, data and photographs to the book and for their untiring efforts in the field (in alphabetical order): Christine Fletcher, Susan Murray, Juliana Senawi, Rakhmad Sujarno, Matthew Struebig, and Tony Wood. Valued contributions to the Megachiroptera accounts came from Robert Hodgkison and Polly Campbell. We gratefully acknowledge the MBCRU logistics team, specifically Zamiza Zainal and James Elder, and the many field assistants from Jah Hut, Che Wong and Malay villages around KWR that have worked with the MBCRU in the past four years. Over 70 volunteers from more than 21 countries have also joined the MBCRU through Earthwatch Institute and Gap Challenge and we greatly appreciate their support of and contribution to the research programme. The book also encompasses the results of over 10 years of collecting and research by DWNP under the direction of Lim Boo Liat, and it is a testimony to the Department's efforts and investment that the bat fauna of Malaysia is one of the best-known in South East Asia.

We are grateful to the Economic Planning Unit of the Malaysian Prime Minister's department for granting permission for Tigga Kingston to conduct wildlife research in Malaysia, the Pahang State Government and to the Director General, Department of Wildlife and National Parks for permission to work at Krau Wildlife Reserve, Pahang. We further thank all at DWNP for their assistance and collaboration. We are indebted to Universiti Kebangsaan Malaysia for their support of the MBCRU and for making it possible to produce this book. Thank you all.

Tigga Kingston
Lim Boo Liat
Zubaid Akbar

1

Introduction

Bats are a vital component of global biodiversity: with 1,111 species worldwide they constitute nearly a fifth of all mammal species (Simmons in press), yet throughout the world populations are declining, ranges contracting and eight species have already become extinct (Mickleburgh et al. 1992; Hutson et al. 2001). Malaysia is a critical country for international bat conservation; it is at the centre of Old World bat diversity (Findley 1993), with over 125 species accounting for over 10% of the world's bat fauna. Forty percent of Malaysian mammals are bats, and in rainforest ecosystems they comprise over half of all mammal species.

Tragically, more than a quarter (34 species) of Malaysian bats are red-listed by IUCN as being at some risk of extinction and many other species are declining; primarily as a result of habitat loss and hunting. This is a great tragedy; not only is Malaysia's bat heritage unique in a global context, but many species play a key role in our daily lives. At least 31 Malaysian plant species rely on bats to pollinate them, including favourites such as durian, petai, mango, banana, guava, jackfruit and papaya. The durian (*Durio* spp.) trade in South East Asia was valued at US$120 million in the mid-1980s (Myers 1985), and sales of petai in the Klang Valley alone generate approximately US$2.8 million annually (Cheun et al. 1998). Old World fruit bats (Megachiroptera) also play an essential ecological and commercial role as seed dispersers (Marshall 1985; Fujita & Tuttle 1991; Shilton et al. 1999), particularly as they frequently move the seeds away from the parent plant where seed predation is high. A botanical survey in just 1 ha of old-growth forest in Krau Wildlife Reserve revealed that 13.7% of trees (greater than or equal to 15 cm girth at breast height) were at least partially dependent upon fruit bats for pollination and/or seed dispersal (Hodgkison et al. 2003a). The insect-eating bats (Microchiroptera) are just as important. Every night, an insectivorous bat needs to eat at least half its body weight in insects. That can be the equivalent of 600 mosquito-sized insects in just an hour, and large colonies can consume over 2,000 tonnes of insects per year.

Within Malaysia, Krau Wildlife Reserve (KWR) comprises 620 km^2 of undisturbed, dipterocarp forest and supports both the best-known bat fauna in the Old World, and the highest diversity of insectivorous bats known for a single site in the world. More than 52 insectivorous species are known from a single 3 km^2 area around Kuala Lompat Field Station (Kingston et al. 2003a; Juliana 2004), one of which is an undescribed *Kerivoula* (Francis et al. in prep) not currently known from any other site in the world. Since 1971, bat research in KWR has generated over 20 publications in national and international journals, two PhD dissertations and three Master's theses. The reserve is the primary study site of the Malaysian Bat Conservation Research Unit (MBCRU). Long-term research by the MBCRU seeks to determine the factors affecting diversity and extinction risk of insectivorous bat communities at the local and landscape scale and provides the basis for a further three PhD and three Master's projects. The plant-visiting Megachiroptera of KWR have also been the subject of one of the most detailed studies in the region (Hodgkison 2001; Hodgkison et al. 2003a, 2003b; Hodgkison et al. 2004a, 2004b), and when the fruit bats and more recent Microchiroptera records are added, species richness for the reserve as a whole rises to a staggering 69 species, 13 of which are on the IUCN Red List. Consequently, KWR is one of the most important areas for bat research and conservation in the Old World tropics and is a critical site for global bat conservation efforts.

The Malaysian Bat Conservation Research Unit (MBCRU)

The MBCRU was established to promote the conservation of Malaysia's unique and threatened bat fauna. It was founded by scientists from the USA (Boston University), Malaysia (Universiti Kebangsaan Malaysia (UKM)), and the Department of Wildlife and National Parks (DWNP) with further collaborations with Queen Mary University of London and University of Bristol, UK, the Malaysian Nature Society, Earthwatch Institute, the Organization for Bat Conservation (OBC) and the Bat Taxon Advisory Group (Bat TAG) of the American Zoo and Aquarium Association. The MBCRU was launched by Musa bin Nordin, the Director

General of DWNP in his opening address to the 12th International Bat Research Conference in Kuala Lumpur, 5th August 2001. The primary objectives of the MBCRU are: long-term research on bat diversity and conservation; capacity building (the development and acquisition of skills and resources in Malaysia through workshops and student support); and implementation of an education programme to highlight the diversity and biology of bats, as well as the international importance of Malaysia to bat conservation.

MBCRU Research Objectives and Study Design

The insectivorous bat species of the rainforest interior are an exceptionally diverse group in Malaysia (Kingston et al. 2003a), and are characterised by specialisations of wing morphology and echolocation signal design that equip them to exploit the abundant prey base of the forest understorey, but greatly constrain their ecological flexibility. They are adept at flying through dense stands of vegetation and use "clutter tolerant" echolocation to pick out prey echoes embedded in those returning from the surrounding vegetation (Schnitzler & Kalko 1998). However, these abilities come at a price; the operating range of clutter-tolerant signals is limited and manouevrable flight is energetically expensive (Kick 1982; Norberg & Rayner 1987; Schnitzler & Kalko 1998), leaving these species ill-suited for prey detection and capture in more open habitats that result from disturbance events, where the dispersed, low-density prey distribution necessitates long-range detection capabilities and fast, efficient flight (Norberg & Rayner 1987; Neuweiler & Fenton 1988; Neuweiler 1990; Schnitzler & Kalko 1998). Consequently, interior species are entirely dependent upon intact expanses of forest and are likely to experience a severe decline in diversity as forest habitats are lost and fragmented (Zubaid 1993).

This inherently vulnerable guild comprises at least 30 species in Malaysia (Kingston et al. 2003a), and the question arises whether some species within this group are more sensitive to disturbance than others. The primary aim of the MBCRU's research is to develop a predictive framework to determine which species within this inherently vulnerable group are at greatest risk of local extinction, so that preventative measures can be implemented before populations decline. Predictors of extinction risk such as abundance, spatial distribution, reproductive phenology, home range, longevity and population turnover rates, and landscape and temporal population variability, are derived from a simple but standardised, spatially-referenced harp-trapping protocol within one of the largest areas of intact lowland rainforest in Peninsular Malaysia, the Krau Wildlife Reserve.

In order to derive landscape-level predictors of extinction risk, sampling is conducted at five study grids a minimum of 7 km apart and all <300 m a.s.l. (Figure 1.1). In addition to a pre-existing network of trails at Kuala Lompat established by Chivers (1980) for primate studies, four

FIGURE 1.1 Map of Krau Wildlife Reserve to show locations of the MBCRU study grids (open shapes) and DWNP field stations where bat surveys have been conducted (filled squares)

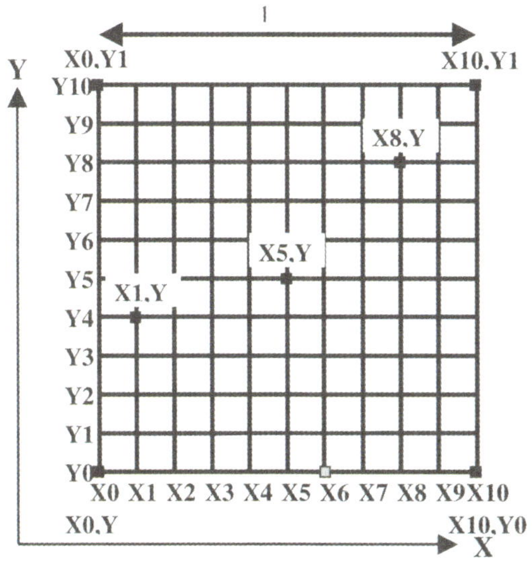

FIGURE 1.2 Design of grids at Kuala Serloh, Jenderak Selatan, Lubuk Baung, and Kuala Gandah. Labeled black squares indicate the name of the intersection; grey square is where the access trail joins the grid at Kuala Gandah (at X6, Y0)

FIGURE 1.3 Four-bank harp trap positioned across a forest trail at Kuala Lompat (Photo Kingston)

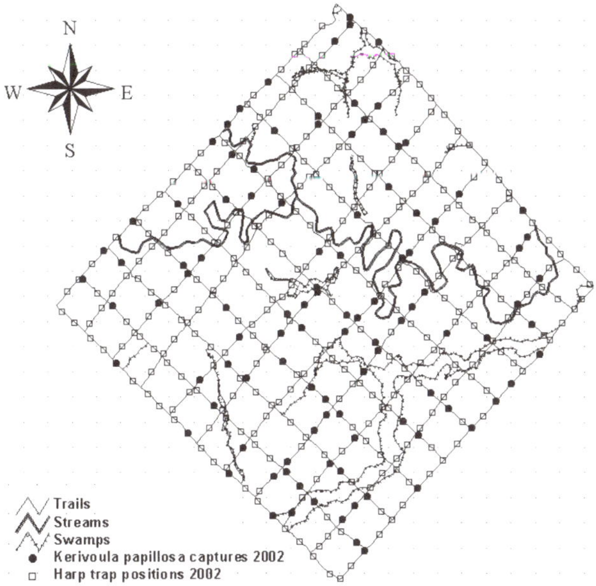

FIGURE 1.4 GIS map of MBCRU grid at Lubuk Baung, showing trails, streams and swamps and distribution of 2002 *Kerivoula papillosa* captures. Clear squares are harp trap positions set in 2002, filled squares are harp traps in which *Kerivoula papillosa* were captured

new sites were developed in 2001/2002: Jenderak Selatan, Kuala Gandah, Kuala Serloh and Lubuk Baung (see Juliana (2004) for details).

Each of the new grids comprises a 1 × 1 km grid with cross trails every 100 m (22 km of trails per grid) (Figure 1.2). Up to 15 four-bank harp traps (Francis 1989) (Figure 1.3) are set during the day, spaced approximately 50 m apart (ca. 435 trap positions per grid per sample, with an offset suite of 435 positions used in alternate years). The traps are checked for bats at 9 pm and then left open over night and re-checked at dawn (following the peaks in bat activity at dusk and dawn). Captured bats are held individually in cloth bags and identified, sexed, weighed, measured and banded with unique wing bands and released at the capture point within 12 hours. All harp trap positions for each grid are mapped and imported into a GIS where they are linked to the capture data (e.g. species, sex, reproductive condition, wing-band number) (Figure 1.3). Individualised capture data generates measures of relative abundance, community composition, longevity, reproductive phenology/seasonality, number of breeding season per year, which combine to influence intrinsic rate of increase. Species distribution patterns and home range indices are derived from the spatially-referenced records. Repeated sampling across the landscape provides a measure of population fluctuations and the extent to which they are spatially autocorrelated and synchronous. Between March 2002 and October 2004 each of the five study grids was sampled twice, generating over 12,500 captures of 42 species (34 Microchiroptera and 8 Megachiroptera). In 2003, we began an extensive radio-tracking programme to determine the impact of roost choice and availability on population processes and extinction risk (Christine Fletcher - Ph.D. dissertation research). A total of 69 individuals of 8 species have been radio-tracked to 218 roosts, all of which have been fully characterised.

2

Using this Field Guide

The guide comprises two parts, a key to the bats of Peninsular Malaysia followed by comprehensive accounts for each of the species recorded for Krau Wildlife Reserve.

Some of the most important tools for biodiversity research and conservation are field guides and systematic keys, but the last comprehensive guide to the bats of Peninsular Malaysia was in Medway (1983), *The Wild Mammals of Malaya (Peninsular Malaysia) and Singapore*. The first edition was published in 1969; with a 2nd edition in 1978 and a reprint with corrections in 1983. Since that time approximately 27 species have been added to the list of species known for Malaysia including nine found in KWR. Consequently, the key includes all species currently known for Peninsular Malaysia, in part because other species may be added to the current list for KWR, but primarily to ensure that the guide has applications beyond the reserve boundaries.

The key is based on external features only, and as such is unlikely to be 100% fool-proof. At certain points the user may need to take specimens to confirm identification through examination of skull parameters, or use alternative non-invasive identification techniques such as genetic or echolocation frequency analyses. The key is largely dichotomous, with occasionally three choices presented. It is advisable to have the relevant measurements ready (forearm length and weight) before beginning to work through the key. As for most keys, the user is often offered several pieces of information at each point in the key. Some diagnostic features are qualitative (e.g., more rounded vs. less rounded) and make more sense if the user is familiar with comparative species. Others are measurements. In general, features that provide the clearest difference between two alternatives should be more reliable (e.g., tibia 13-15 mm vs. tibia 16-18 mm), and generally we have tried to present these first in the dichotomy. Measurements based on bones (forearm, tibia) are easier to measure consistently than those based on soft tissue (ears). Photographic illustrations of the key diagnostic features are given wherever possible. However, the user should be aware that colour and fine detail of the structures may vary from species to species.

When a candidate species has been identified, the user should refer to the species account if the bat comes from KWR, or consult Medway (1983) or Payne and Francis (1985). These accounts provide more details of the species and can confirm identifications. Note that if the species account was based on only a few specimens it is possible that some measurements may be outside the range given, particularly if this is derived from data collected in a different geographical location (e.g. forearm lengths for specimens from Borneo may differ slightly from those on the Peninsula). If the identification remains a poor match with the species account, the key should be revisited and each dichotomous choice checked. Was there one choice that was questionable? If it is still not possible to resolve between two candidate species, then a specimen should be collected.

Species Accounts

Given that it has been more than twenty years since Medway's (1983) account of the bat fauna of Peninsular Malaysia, we have tried to make the species accounts as comprehensive as possible. We have consequently drawn on all published information available for the species in Malaysia, but the emphasis remains on data derived from research conducted at KWR. The accounts include the following:

Species name: Follows Simmons (in press) for nomenclature and English name. Where this nomenclature differs from that used by Medway (1983) or Corbet and Hill (1992), the former names are given in parentheses. Malay names are also given, but in many cases these are literal translations of the English name and are not widely used.

Description: Wherever possible, this is based on live animals and indicates key diagnostic features that distinguish the species from similar congenerics.

Measurements: Two data sources are given:

1 Specimen data, primarily from the collection held at the Department of Wildlife and National Parks (specimens from throughout Peninsular Malaysia) but with additional data from the MBCRU collection from KWR at Universiti Kebangsaan Malaysia. The measurements given are those typically used for Chiroptera specimen data and refer to adults only:
HB: head and body (mm) - from the anus to the front of the nose.
T: tail (mm) - distance from the base of the tail just below the anus to the tip of the last caudal vertebra (tail bone).
FA: forearm (mm) - from the outside of the elbow to the outside of the wrist in the bent wing. Measured with calipers, the elbow is placed on the broadest part of the moveable lower jaw of the calipers and closed and adjusted until the fixed upper jaw contacts the wrist. The bone is parallel to the long axis of the calipers; if the bone is naturally curved, the wrist and elbow are in line.
Tb: tibia (mm) - from the ankle to the tip of the knee.
E: ear height (mm) - from the notch at the base of the ear to the tip of the ear.
Wt: weight (g) - excluding pregnant females.

2 FA and Wt from live animals captured regularly at KWR by the MBCRU, or published in Kingston et al. (2003a) or Hodgkison (2001). Weights of live bats are most easily obtained if the animal is wrapped inside a section of women's stocking (easily manipulated and the bat does not struggle). Weights are taken to 0.5 g with a spring balance.

Echolocation: Published accounts of descriptive signal parameters, or unpublished data from current research conducted by the MBCRU (primarily the work of T. Wood, per. com.). Many of these data come from recordings at KWR, or, unless otherwise stated, from Peninsular Malaysia (as geographic variation in call frequency can be substantial in some species).

Ecology: What is known of the ecology of the species from studies within the reserve and throughout Malaysia.

Breeding: Reproductive phenology data from three sources:

1 Dissection of specimens that are part of the DWNP collection (so could have originated outside of the reserve) or MBCRU collection.

This is the most accurate assessment of pregnancy.

2 Field data from the MBCRU project at KWR between March 2002 and September 2004 (excluding November and December for each year) are also given. For the Megachiroptera, we include data collected at Kuala Lompat over two 12-month seasons between May 1997 and November 1999 by Hodgkison (2001). Females are identified as lactating if milk can be expressed from the nipple by gentle palpation, and mammary glands appear white (Figure 2.1). Late stage pregnancy can be judged by gently feeling the abdominal area of a distended female to detect the skull of the foetus (Figure 2.2). The latter can be more difficult to distinguish, particularly in small bats that have been captured just after eating, and consequently, the lactation data are given first.

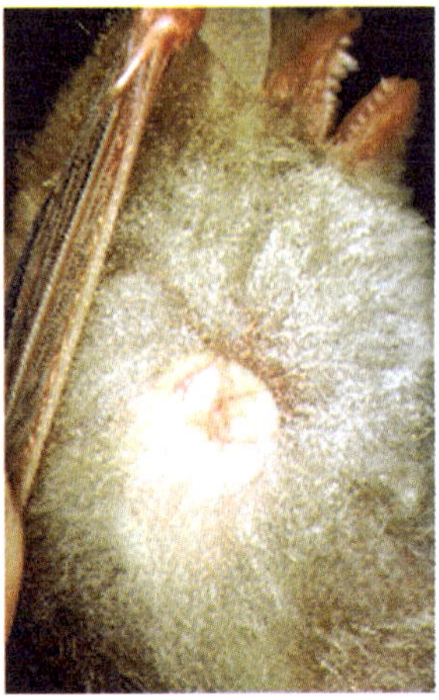

FIGURE 2.1 Right mammary gland of *Kerivoula pellucida* during lactation (Photo Kingston)

3 Published accounts of reproductive phenology and/or characteristics such as gestation and lactation periods.

FIGURE 2.2 Late pregnancy in *Hipposideros diadema*

IUCN: Designation of species by IUCN as of 2002.

Threatened categories:

VU - vulnerable

B - extent of occurrence <20,000 km^2 or area of occupancy <2,000 km^2 AND

1 - population severely fragmented or known to occur in no more than 10 locations.

2c - continuing decline in area/extent/quality of habitat observed/inferred or projected.

Lower risk categories:

LR(nt) - near threatened.

LR(lc) - least concern.

DD - Data Deficient. Inadequate information to make a direct or indirect assessment of species risk of extinction based on its distribution and/or population status.

Distribution KWR: Distribution data for KWR from three sources:

1 Field data from the MBCRU project at KWR between March 2002 and October 2004. During this period each grid was surveyed with harp traps (for approximately 435 harp trap nights per grid) twice, generating over 12,500 captures comprising 42 species (34 Microchiroptera, 8 Megachiroptera (Kingston et al. in press). The numbers of individuals and recaptures are given for each of the five MBCRU study sites (Jenderak Selatan, Kuala Gandah, Kuala Lompat, Kuala Serloh and Lubuk Baung). Harp traps are biased towards forest interior insectivorous bats of the families Hipposideridae and Rhinolophidae and the two vespertilionid subfamilies Murininae and Kerivoulinae. The data are therefore presumed to provide an accurate representation of the abundance and distribution of species in these taxa, but bats of other insectivorous families (Molossidae, Vespertilionidae (subfamilies Vespertilioninae and Miniopterinae) and the plant-visiting Pteropodidae will be under-represented.

2 DWNP specimen records, compiled by Lim Boo Liat.

3 Field data from the MBCRU gathered by other means: mist netting over rivers, off-grid harp trap captures, cave visits, or records of note during the initial stages of the third round of trapping by the MBCRU (January 2005 onwards).

4 Observations and records of other researchers, most notably the work of Robert Hodgkison on the Megachiroptera at Kuala Lompat between May 1997 and November 1999.

Distribution: Global distribution following Simmons (in press).

3

Field Guide to the Bats of Krau Wildlife Reserve

Key to the Bats of Peninsular Malaysia

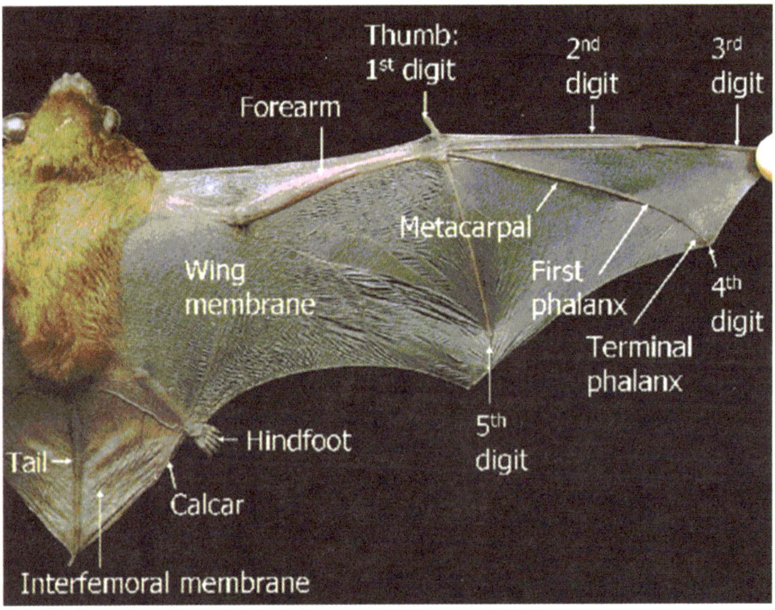

FIGURE 3.1 Dorsal view of *Scotophilus kuhlii* to show parts of a bat (Photo Wood)

Key to Families

1 Claw on 2nd digit (except *Eonycteris*); simple ears with outer margins forming an unbreakable ring; dog- or fox-like face; FA 40-220 mm PTEROPODIDAE

No claw on 2nd digit; ears often complex with tragus; face not dog-like 2

2 Tail ends in a T-or V-shaped cartilage enclosed in interfemoral membrane (Figure 3.2); deep slit in face, ears large, separated at base NYCTERIDAE

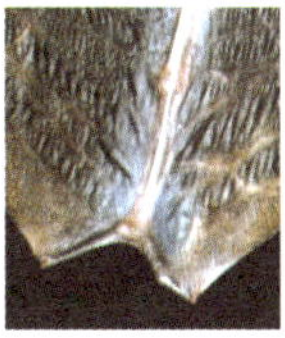

FIGURE 3.2

Tail does not end in a T-shaped cartilage, no deep slit in face 3

3 Tail extends for at least half its length beyond the end of interfemoral membrane (Figure 3.3) MOLOSSIDAE

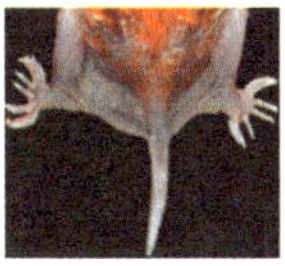

FIGURE 3.3

Tail is shorter than the interfemoral membrane and protrudes from the middle of the dorsal side of the membrane (Figure 3.4) EMBALLONURIDAE

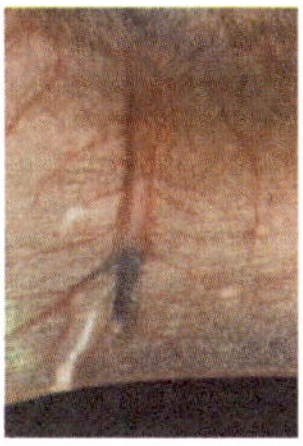

FIGURE 3.4

Tail, if present, is fully enclosed in interfemoral membrane (tip may just appear to extend beyond, but is within the membrane) (Figure 3.5) 4

FIGURE 3.5

4 Plain nose VESPERTILIONIDAE

Leaf-like structure on nose and face 5

5 Tragus long and bifurcate (Figure 3.6); large rounded ears joined across top of head; upper incisors lacking MEGADERMATIDAE

Tragus simple; ears not joined across top of head; upper incisors present 6

FIGURE 3.6

6 Median noseleaf (behind nostrils) has a raised portion, the sella; posterior noseleaf rises to a long lancet-shaped point (Figures 3.7, 3.13); ears with pronounced antitragus — RHINOLOPHIDAE

FIGURE 3.7

Median leaf is a low cushion-like structure expanded laterally without a sella; posterior leaf is low and rounded, usually divided by vertical septa into several pockets (Figures 3.8, 3.16); ears with low antitragus — HIPPOSIDERIDAE

FIGURE 3.8

Pteropodidae

- simple ears with outer margins forming an unbroken ring
- dog- or fox-like face
- FA 40-220 mm
- tail short or lacking, when present not involved with membrane
- interfemoral membrane narrow
- simple cusps

1 Claw present on 2nd finger (Figure 3.9) — 2

No claw on 2nd finger — *Eonycteris spelaea*

2 Large; FA > 120 mm; Wt > 200 g — *Pteropus* 3

Small-medium; FA < 90 mm — 4

3 FA 170-210 mm; Wt > 700 g — *Pteropus vampyrus*

FA 130-150 mm; Wt < 300 g — *Pteropus hypomelanus*

4 Tail distinct — 5

Tail indistinct or lacking — 11

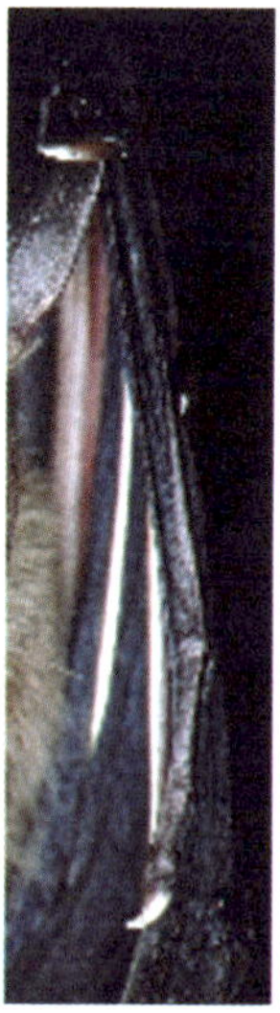

FIGURE 3.9

5 2 pairs of lower incisors 6

1 pair of lower incisors *Penthetor lucasi*

6 Skull compact with short rostrum (short stout muzzle), 3/4 upper cheek teeth, 5 lower 8

Muzzle fairly long; 5 upper, 6 lower cheek teeth *Rousettus* 7

7 Uniformly dark brown; ear width 12-13 mm; lower last molar subcircular *Rousettus amplexicaudatus*

Lighter brown; ear width 14.5-15.5 mm, lower last molar elliptical; in P. Malaysia only known from skulls in Batu caves *Rousettus leschenaultii*

8 Ears not edged with white; 3 upper cheek teeth; cheek teeth greatly enlarged, squarish with large cusps and ridge *Dyacopterus spadiceus*

Ears hairless and edged with white; 4 upper cheek teeth; anterior premolar very small; *Cynopterus* 9

9 FA < 65 mm *Cynopterus brachyotis*

FA > 65 mm 10

10 FA 65-74 mm; Wt 33-67 g; no peg-like cusps on lower cheek teeth *Cynopterus sphinx*

FA 70-80 mm; Wt 57-74 g; peg-like cusp on lower cheek teeth *Cynopterus horsfieldii*

11 Skull fairly compact with short muzzle 13

Narrow muzzle; very long tongue *Macroglossus* 12

12 Internarial groove extending to upper lip *Macroglossus minimus*

Groove does not bisect upper lip, lower jaw is longer creating an under bite *Macroglossus sobrinus*

13 1 pair lower incisors 14

2 pairs of lower incisors; black cap to head *Chironax melanocephalus*

14 Pale spots on wings; FA < 45 mm; 5 upper molars, extra one very small *Balionycteris maculata*

No pale spots on wings; FA > 45 mm; 4 upper molars 15

15 Nostrils normal; FA 45-50 mm; interfemoral membrane thickly furred; generally dark colour *Aethalops alecto*

Tubular nostrils; FA 51-58 mm; interfemoral membrane thinly furred; fawn to pale grey *Megaerops* 16

16 FA 45-52 mm; Tb < 15 mm; large white tufts on side of neck create a broken collar *Megaerops wetmorei*

FA 50-60 mm; Tb > 15 mm; upperparts yellowish-brown to pale grey, underparts paler *Megaerops ecaudatus*

Emballonuridae

- small to large
- variable ears, often joined anteriorly at the base over the forehead
- small or moderate tragus
- no noseleaf
- glandular pouch or beard may be present on throat
- tail partly enclosed in moderate tail membrane, its terminal part projecting from the upper surface

1 FA < 50 mm *Emballonura monticola*

FA > 50 mm 2

2 Radio-metacarpal pouch absent or poorly developed; Wt > 35 g; chin naked, male with throat pouch (Figure 3.10); legs naked/sparsely furred *Saccolaimus saccolaimus*

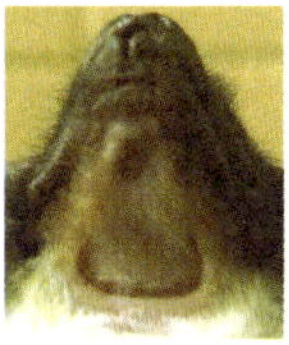

FIGURE 3.10

Radio-metacarpal pouch present (Figure 3.11); Wt < 35 g; legs and feet with short fur 3

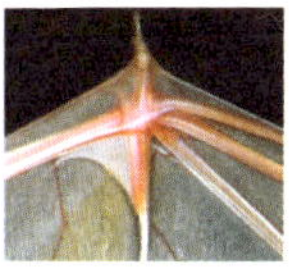

FIGURE 3.11

3 FA 63-68 mm; chin furred, male with dark brown hairs on underside of chin *Taphozous melanopogon*

FA 54-58 mm; chin naked, male with throat pouch *Taphozous longimanus*

Nycteridae

- medium to large
- v. long ears separated at base
- short rounded tragus
- long tail with T- or V-shaped tip fully enclosed in interfemoral membrane
- face has deep groove in middle bordered by leaf-like flaps of skin

- *Nycteris* is the sole genus, and *Nycteris tragata* the only Malaysian species

Megadermatidae

- medium to large
- large erect noseleaf
- large ears joined across the top of the head by a band of integument
- tragus long and forked (bifurcated)
- very short tail, not visible externally, but interfemoral membrane well developed

1 FA > 65 mm; Tb > 36 mm; Wt 40 g; intermediate noseleaf narrow, sub-circular; posterior leaf subrectangular, flattened above *Megaderma lyra*

FA < 60 mm; Tb < 35 mm; Wt < 30 g; intermediate noseleaf broad, chordate; posterior broadly elliptical, slightly rounded above *Megaderma spasma*

Rhinolophidae

- small-medium size
- elaborate noseleaf: anterior section is rounded and roughly horse-shoe-shaped; behind the nostrils is a raised portion - the sella; behind this is a posterior noseleaf which rises to a long, lancet-shaped point (Figure 3.12).
- ears large with prominent anti tragus

1 Sella bears lateral processes *philippinensis group* 2

Sella without lateral processes 6

2 Sella with lateral lappets, making it appear trifid (Figure 3.12) 4

No lateral lappets, sella does not appear trifid 3

3 Internarial septum greatly expanded to form wing-like structure integral to base of sella; connecting process low and joins sella with no notch; lancet low, triangular, rounded tip *R. marshalli*

Internarial septum normal; lateral processes of sella join expanded margins of the nostrils to form an internarial bowl-shaped structure; connecting process high with notch where it joins sella; constant frequency (CF) portion of the echolocation call 48 kHz *R. macrotis*

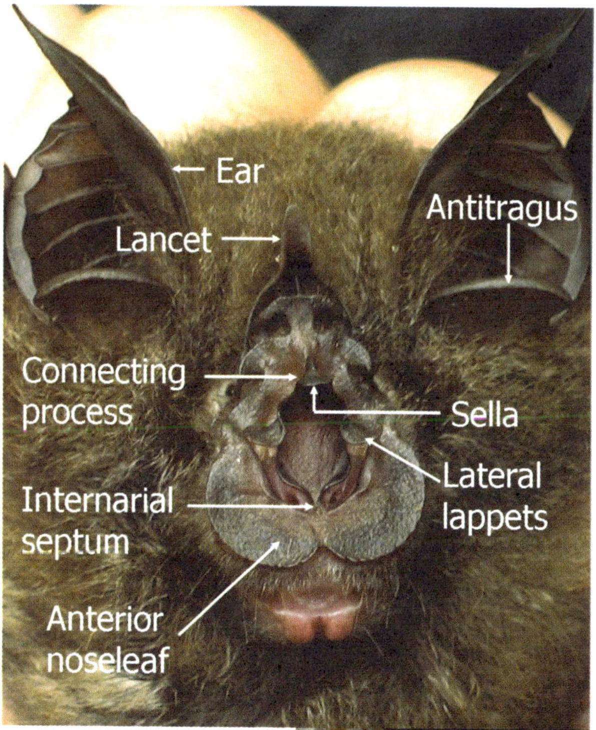

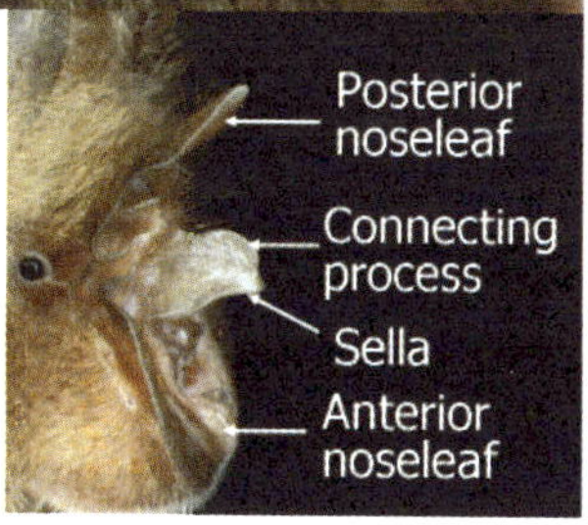

FIGURE 3.12 Noseleaf of *Rhinolophus* showing names of parts. Anterior view of face of *Rhinolophus luctus* (above) (Photo Struebig) and lateral view of noseleaf of *Rhinolophus stheno* (Photo Kingston)

4 Noseleaf and ears yellow; FA 45-56 mm; CF 53 kHz *R. trifoliatus*

Noseleaf and ears dark grey/brown 5

5 FA 37-44 mm; Wt 7-10 g; CF 67 kHz *R. sedulus*

FA 63-67 mm; Wt 26-37 g; CF 42 kHz *R. luctus*

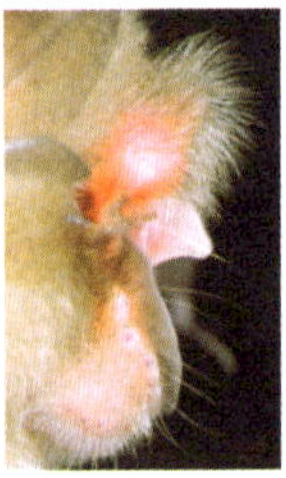

FIGURE 3.13

6 Posterior noseleaf projecting forward to enclose base of connecting process - connecting process inserted into a fissure of the thickened lancet; lancet densely haired (Figure 3.13) *R. coelophyllus/shameli*

N.B. Difficult to distinguish between *coelophyllus* and *shameli* externally

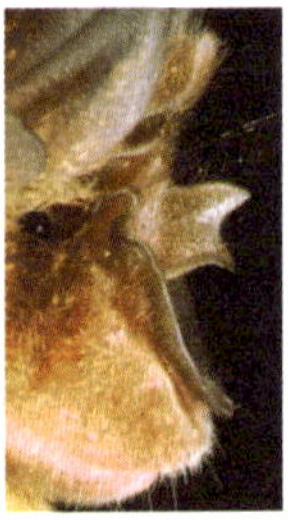

FIGURE 3.14

Rear of connecting process attached directly to face of posterior leaf, not enclosed 7

7 Connecting process rounded (Figure 3.12) *ferrumequinum* group 8

Connecting process triangular, pointed (Figure 3.14) *pusillus (lepidus)* group 11

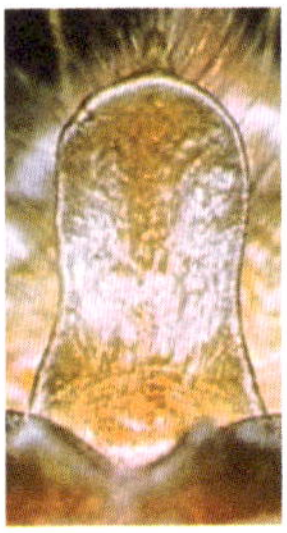

FIGURE 3.15

8 Upright part of sella with parallel sides 9

Upright part of sella concave (Figure 3.15) or with step-wise constriction (Figure 3.16) 10

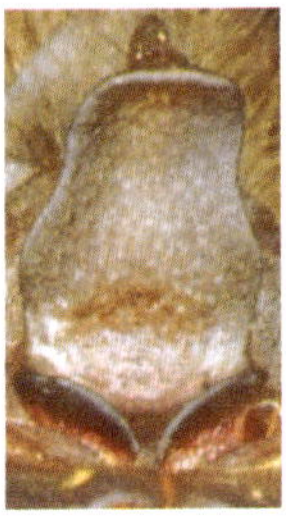

FIGURE 3.16

9 FA 39-43 mm; Tb 17-18 mm; Wt 4-6 g; CF 75 kHz; 2nd phalanx of 3rd finger < 1x length of 1st finger *R. malayanus*

FA 43-49 mm; Tb 19-22 mm; Wt 6-12 g; CF 86 kHz, 2nd phalanx of 3rd finger > 1.5x length of 1st finger *R. stheno*

N.B. Watch for *R. borneensis* FA 40-44 mm, Wt 7-8 g. The lancet is bluntly pointed and straight-sided unlike the long sharply-pointed lance of *R. malayanus*.

10 Upright part of sella wider at base than at tip, with a step-wise constriction at mid-length (Figure 3.16); FA 40-44 mm; Wt 8-9 g; CF 67 kHz *R. robinsoni*

N.B. May see *R. robinsoni* as *R. megaphyllus* but incorrect

Sella with concave sides (Figure 3.15); FA 48-54 mm; Wt 12-17 g; CF 78 kHz *R. affinis*

11 FA 45-53 mm *R. acuminatus*

FA < 44 mm 12

12 Connecting process is slender and projects anteriorly far beyond the tip of the sella; widely rounded lancet *R. convexus*

Connecting process does not project beyond the tip of sella 13

13 Lancet broadly pointed; connecting process less pointed; FA 36-43 mm; E 16-17 mm; CF 100 kHz; tips of hairs paler *R. lepidus (refulgens)*

Lancet sharply pointed; connecting process more pointed; FA 37-40 mm; E 13-16 mm *R. pusillus*

Hipposideridae

- small to moderately large
- elaborate noseleaf: anterior noseleaf is rounded and somewhat horse-shoe-shaped (except in *Coelops*); median leaf is a low cushion-like structure expanded laterally without a sella; posterior leaf is low and rounded, usually divided by vertical septa into several pockets; some species have lateral leaflets below anterior noseleaf
- low antitragus
- eyes very small

1 Upper margin of posterior noseleaf divided into three distinct points FA 39-44 mm *Aselliscus stoliczkanus*

Not divided 2

2 Deep notch in anterior noseleaf which is expanded to the sides (Figure 3.17); no visible tail, but extensive interfemoral membrane *Coelops* 3

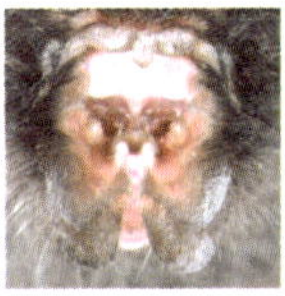

FIGURE 3.17

Typical horseshoe-shaped anterior noseleaf (Figure 3.18); tail short-moderate, largely enclosed in interfemoral membrane *Hipposideros* 4

3 FA 34-37 mm; noseleaf with wide rounded lappets projecting from the supplementary leaflets *Coelops robinsoni*

FA 43-47 mm; noseleaf with elongated narrow lappets projecting from the supplementary leaflets *Coelops frithii*

4 Fleshy outgrowth behind posterior noseleaf 5

No additional structures behind posterior noseleaf 6

5 FA 71-84 mm; transverse accessory bilobed struc-

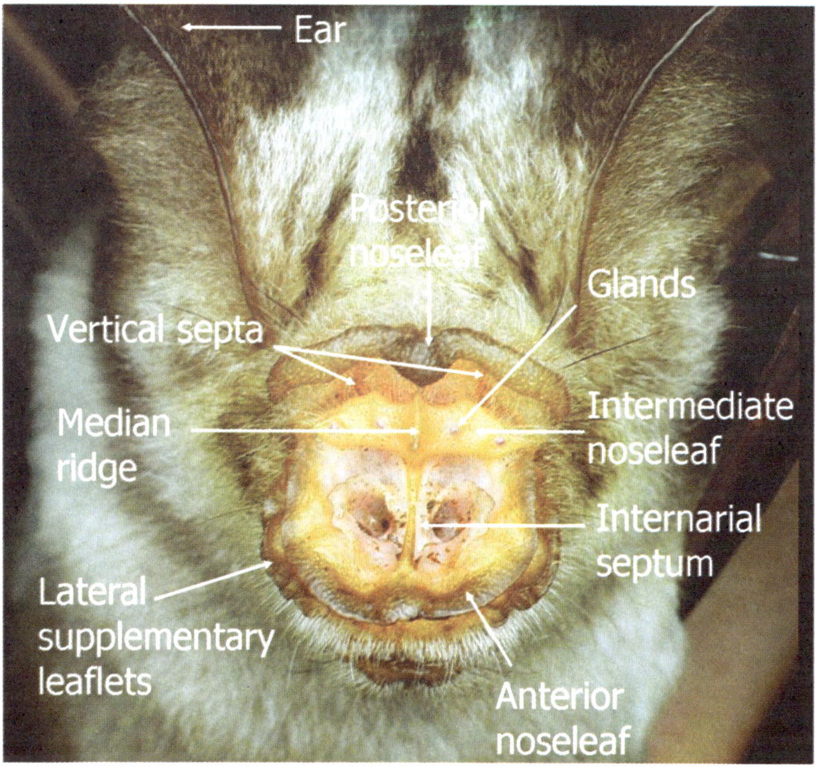

FIGURE 3.18 Anterior view of noseleaf and face of *Hipposideros* to show naming of parts (Photo Kingston)

ture behind posterior leaf, (especially in males (Figure 3.19)); no lateral leaflets
Hipposideros lylei

FIGURE 3.19

FA 88-98 mm; outgrowths smaller, not bilobed; upper margins of posterior leaf thickened and developed into 3 rounded lobes (Figure 3.20); 4 lateral leaflets *H. armiger*

FIGURE 3.20

6 2-4 lateral leaflets present 7

No lateral leaflets 10

7 FA > 55 mm 8

FA < 53 mm 9

8 FA 79-90 mm; 3 lateral leaflets; upperparts light brown with which or cream blaze over shoulder CF 60 kHz *H. diadema*

FA 71-80 mm; upper part of posterior noseleaf heavily lobulated *H. lekaguli*

FA 57-61 mm; 3 lateral leaflets; uniform brown/ orange; CF 100 kHz *H. larvatus*

9 Intermediate noseleaf wider than posterior; tail > 30 mm *H. galeritus*

Intermediate noseleaf narrower than posterior; tail 21-28 mm; CF 126 kHz *H. cervinus*

FIGURE 3.21

10 Disk-like structure in internarial region of noseleaf, covering external nares (Figure 3.21) 11

No such disk 12

11 E 20.9-23.9 mm; small internarial disk (1.9-2.4 mm), not completely rounded and joins anterior noseleaf at base; 80 kHz *H. orbiculus*

E 22.0-25.6 mm; large internarial disk (3.0-3.4 mm), completely rounded with complete margin free of anterior noseleaf; 62 kHz *H. ridleyi*

12 Posterior noseleaf has no septa, concave surface is smooth; FA 33-38 mm; Wt 4-6 g; CF 195 kHz *H. doriae* (*sabanus*)

Posterior noseleaf with 3 septa dividing concave face into 4 equal sized cells 13

13 Noseleaf dark, ears broadly triangular (view top half of ear in isolation) (Figure 3.22); FA 38-42 mm *H. dyacorum*

Noseleaf pinkish, ears rounded 14

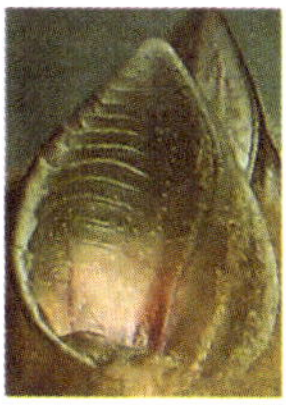

FIGURE 3.22

14 Internarial septum slightly swollen in middle (Figure 3.23); FA 36-41 mm; E 18.5-21.0 mm; 4-6 g; CF 144 kHz *H. cineraceus*

FIGURE 3.23

Internarial septum slightly swollen at base and very narrow in middle; FA 39-43 mm; E 15.0-17.5 mm; Wt 5-8 g (CF 166 kHz - India) *H. ater*

Internarial septum straight (Figure 3.24); FA 41-47 mm; 7-9 g 15

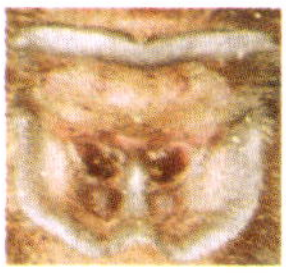

FIGURE 3.24

15 Ear very large, 20-23 mm *H. pomona*

Ear smaller, 17-21 mm 16

16 FA < 43 mm; Tb < 19 mm; noseleaf and ears slightly blacker; CF c. 142 kHz *H. bicolor* 142

FA > 45 mm; Tb > 20 mm; paler 'flatter' anterior noseleaf; CF c. 131 kHz *H. bicolor* 131

N.B. FA 43-45 mm; or Tb 19-20 mm; not possible to distinguish between species without call frequency

N.B. Watch out for *H. nequam* with NL 6x8 instead of 5x6 mm known from a single specimen collected at Klang, Selangor.

Vespertilionidae

- nose simple without noseleaf (Malaysian species)
- ears small to large with a well-developed tragus
- tail long and completely enclosed in the interfemoral membrane

Subfamilies of Vespertilionidae

1 Nostrils laterally elongated, tubular in form; extending beyond upper lip and opening at sides (Figure 3.25) MURININAE

Nostrils not tubular 2

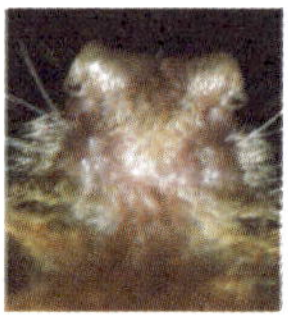

FIGURE 3.25

2 Ears funnel-shaped with long, pointed tragus (Figure 3.26) KERIVOULINAE

Ears normal 3

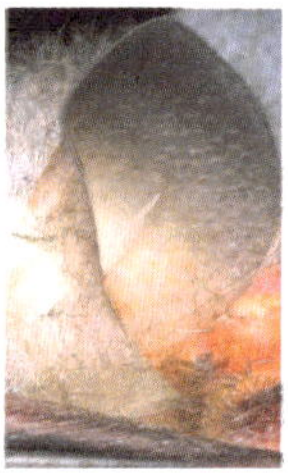

FIGURE 3.26

3 Proximal phalanx of 3rd digit < 40% of length of terminal phalanx so that wing at rest bends up (N.B. from the wrist order of bones in the hand are: metacarpal, proximal phalanx, terminal phalanx) MINIOPTERINAE

Proximal phalanx of 3rd digit approximately same length as terminal phalanx VESPERTILIONINAE

Murininae

1 FA > 45 mm; 3rd upper molar (M^3) tiny, sometimes lacking; bright orange *Harpiocephalus mordax*

FA < 40 mm; M^3 well developed *Murina* 2

2 Fur on back pale brown or orange, not tipped with colour 3

Fur on back dark, tipped with colour (Figure 3.27) 4

FIGURE 3.27

3 FA 28-32 mm; E 10-13 mm; Wt 3.0-5.5 g; upperparts buffy brown/orange, underparts greyish-white *M. suilla*

FA 32-36 mm, E 16-17 mm; Wt 5.5-7.5 g (smaller version of *M. cyclotis* with large ears - rare) *M. huttoni*

FA 33-38 mm; E 11-15 mm; Wt 6.5-12.0 g *M. cyclotis*

4 FA 28-32 mm; Wt 4-5 g; shining yellow-golden tips to dark fur; underparts slightly paler *M. rozendaali*

FA 34-38 mm; Wt 6.0-8.5 g; orange-brown tips to dark fur; underparts whitish *M. aenea*

Kerivoulinae

1 Tragus with distinct notch in posterior margin near base (Figure 3.28); upper canines with longitudinal grooves on outer faces *Phoniscus* 2

No notch in tragus; canines ungrooved *Kerivoula* 3

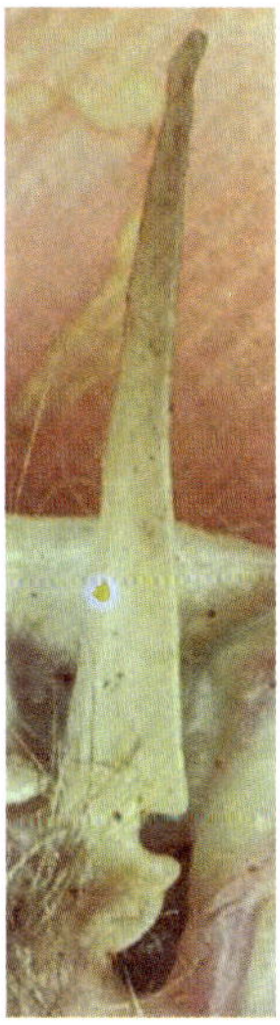

FIGURE 3.28

2 FA 37-43 mm; Wt 9-10 g; hairs banded black and white with pale golden tips *P. jagorii*

FA 30-36 mm; Wt 4-5.5 g; hairs with golden/bronze tips *P. atrox*

3 Wings orange and black; FA 34-39 mm *K. picta*

Wings semi-translucent; FA 28-33 mm; fur on upperparts buffy-brown with pale bases; face and ears yellow-pink *K. pellucida*

Wings normal brown 4

4 Fur on upperparts dark brown at base with gold/bronze tips; FA 28-32 mm, Wt 2.5-3 g *K. sp*

Fur orange or brown or grey-brown without gold tips 5

5 Fur orange-brown with slatey-grey bases 6

Fur brown or pale buffy-brown or greyish 7

6 FA 25-30 mm; Wt 2.0-2.5 g *K. minuta*

FA 26-32 mm; Wt 2.5-5.0 g *K. intermedia*

N.B. Differentiation between *K. minuta* and *K. intermedia* very difficult, and these FA and Wt criteria are somewhat arbitrary. *K. intermedia* differs from *whiteheadi* in colour and premolar shape

7 FA 28-29 mm; tips of the wings white; 2nd and 3rd premolars elongate and oval in cross section; upperparts pale brown with dark grey bases; underparts greyish white *K. whiteheadi*

FA 31-34 mm; Tb 16-18 mm; greyish brown fur *K. hardwickii*

FA 37-45 mm; Tb 18-25 mm *K. papillosa*

Miniopterinae

FA 47-52 mm; Tb 20.0-21.5 mm; Wt 13-16 g *Miniopterus magnater*

FA 42-50 mm; Tb 16-18 mm; Wt 10-15 g (usually smaller than *magnater*) *M. schreibersii*

FA 35-42 mm; Tb 16-17 mm; Wt 7-11 g *M. medius*

Vespertilioninae

1 1 pair of upper incisors *Scotophilus kuhlii*

2 pairs of upper incisors, 1st v. large and conical and about half size of canine, 2nd small and may be displaced inwards; only 1 upper premolar *Hesperoptenus* 2

2 pairs of upper incisors, normal 4

2 FA > 47-52 mm *Hesperoptenus tomesi*

FA < 45 mm 3

3 FA 38-41 mm; 2nd incisor inline with toothrow *H. doriae*

FA 24-29 mm; 2nd incisor displaced inwards; slight kidney- shaped thickening at base of thumb *H. blanfordi*

4 Thickened pad at wrist and foot 5

No pad 7

5 Pads brown and circular (Figure 3.29) *Tylonycteris* 6

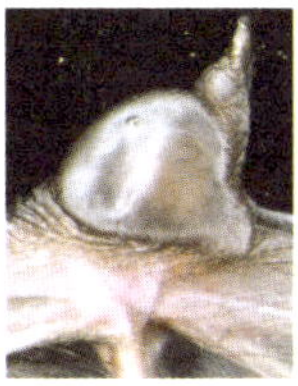

FIGURE 3.29

Pads unpigmented (white/pink) and kidney-shaped; 2nd upper incisor displaced outwards so that the two lie in line *Glischropus tylopus*

6 FA 24-31 mm; Wt 3.5-5.0 g *Tylonycteris pachypus*

FA 27-33 mm; Wt 7-10 g *T. robustula*

FIGURE 3.30

7 Tragus long, slender, bluntly pointed, more or less straight, its length along the anterior margin at least 3x times its greatest width (Figure 3.30); cheek teeth usually 6/6 (except *M. ridleyi* 5/6) *Myotis* 8

Tragus shorter, wider, generally rounded at tip, usually curved forwards, its length along the anterior margin usually less than 3x its greatest width (Figure 3.31); cheek teeth fewer than 6/6 15

FIGURE 3.31

8 Wing, forearm and interfemoral membrane conspicuously parti-coloured black and orange; fur orange; FA 65 mm; Wt 16 g
subgenus *Chrysopteron* - *Myotis hermani*

N.B. Simmons (in press) does not include *M. hermani* in *formosus*, and lists the distribution of *hermani* as Sumatra, with that of *formosus* extending to Afghanistan and Sulawesi.

Wings brown or black; FA < 45 mm 9

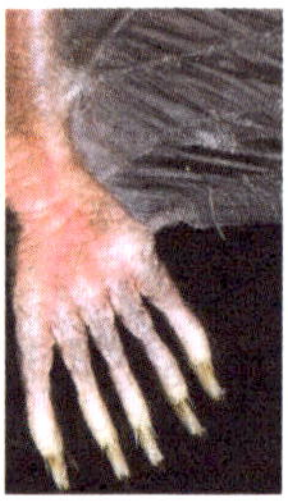

FIGURE 3.32

9 Small feet (< ½ length of tibia); wing membrane attached at base of toes (Figure 3.32)
subgenus *Selysius* 10

FIGURE 3.33

Large feet (½ - ¾ length of tibia) (Figure 3.33); wing membrane attached to ankle or side of foot (> 1 mm from base of toes)
subgenus *Leuconoe* 13

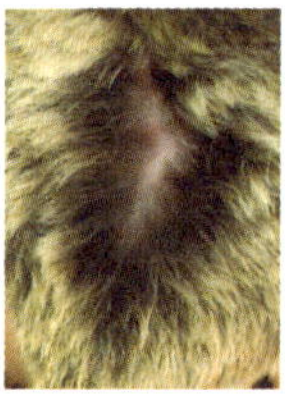

FIGURE 3.34

10 Large, FA 41-48 mm; Tb 16.5-17.5 mm; Wt 9.0-13.5 g; dark upperparts, lower with paler tips (Figure 3.34)
Myotis montivagus

Medium, FA 33-42 mm 11

Small FA 27-33 mm (v. occasionally get larger *M. ridleyi*) 12

11 Larger, FA 34-39 mm; Wt 5-8 g; 2nd premolar v. small and displaced inwards; posterior upper premolar as long as canine; dark upperparts with slightly glossy tips, paler under with long black bases and buffy brown tips *M. ater*

Smaller, FA 33-36 mm; Wt 4-5.5 g; 2nd upper premolar not displaced inwards; canines longer than premolars; upper brown to grey *M. muricola*

12 Small and light; FA 28-33 mm; Wt 2-3 g; 3 premolars *M. siligorensis*

Small and heavy; FA 27-35 mm; Wt 4.0-6.5 g, 2 premolars, dark fur 'chunky' *M. ridleyi*

13 Wing membrane attached to side of foot (at least 1 mm up from base of toes); FA 35-38 mm; Wt 5-7 g; dorsal pelage with tricoloured hairs *M. horsfieldii*

Membrane attached to ankle 14

14 FA 34-37 mm; fur short and velvety; 2nd upper premolar v. small and displaced inwards so 1st and 3rd premolars are in contact or nearly so; base of thumb with small pad *M. hasseltii*

FA 39-40 mm; fur long and woolly; 2nd upper premolar not much smaller than 1st, in line (or nearly) with other premolars *M. adversus*

15 Inner upper incisor long and narrow with 2 cusps; canine with distinct posterior supplementary cusp extending from a third to half its length; one upper premolar; external genitalia quite elaborate; FA < 36 mm *Philetor brachypterus*

Inner upper incisor rounded; no canine cusp; 2 upper premolars 16

16 Large FA 39-42 mm; Wt 18-20 g; wing narrow with short 5th finger (metacarpal short); reddish-brown *Pipistrellus stenopterus*

Wt < 15 g; metacarpal of 5th finger as long as or only a little shorter than that of 4th digit 17

17 Upperparts v. dark brown, hairs tipped with orange or gold 18

Upperpart hairs not orange tipped 19

18 FA 38-44 mm; Tb 18-22 mm; Wt 8-11 g
Arielulus circumdatus

FA 35-39 mm; Tb 14-15 mm; Wt 4.3 -5.5 g
Arielulus societatis

19 Narrow diastema between outer upper incisor and canine 20

Outer upper incisor in contact with canine; 1st upper premolar v. small and displaced inwards from toothrow so canine in contact with 2nd premolar; FA 33-37 mm
Hypsugo macrotis/imbricatus

N.B. *H. macrotis* sometimes listed as subspecies of *H. imbricatus*. Simmons (in press) treats them as separate species with *H. macrotis* in P. Malaysia and *H. imbricatus* in Borneo

20 FA 31-38 mm; Tb 12-14 mm; Wt 3.8-4.7 g; dark brown *Pipistrellus javanicus*

FA 26-32 mm; Tb 11-13 mm; Wt 3-4 g; blackish
P. tenuis

Molossidae

- thickened tail protrudes from end of interfemoral membrane
- no noseleaf, muzzle projects well beyond lower jaw
- lips often somewhat wrinkled
- ears thick, sometimes joined over top of head by a band of skin

1 Large (FA > 70 mm); naked, only scattered hairs
Cheiromeles torquatus

Smaller (FA < 50 mm); fur thick and short 2

2 4 upper cheek teeth (lacks small anterior premolar); M^3 (last molar) reduced or flattened antero-posteriorly *Mops mops*

5 upper cheek teeth (small unicuspid anterior molar), M^3 normal *Chaerephon* 3

3 Upper border of band of skin uniting ears is raised at centre to form a lid covering an enclosed groove or pocket between the ears *Chaerephon johorensis*

No interaural pocket, and interaural band of skin is narrow and not extended vertically *Chaerephon plicata*

Species Accounts

Suborder Megachiroptera
Family Pteropodidae - Old World Fruit Bats

The suborder Megachiroptera comprises a single family of plant-visiting bats, the Pteropodidae, and in Peninsular Malaysia is represented by 17 species from 11 genera, of which 11 species have been recorded for Krau Wildlife Reserve. The most distinctive characteristic of this suborder is the ear margin which forms a continuous ring around the ear. In all species except the Lesser Dawn Bat (*Eonycteris spelaea*) the second digit bears a claw. The face is dog-like, and the tail short or lacking, and when present is not involved with the interfemoral membrane, which is narrow.

Balionycteris maculata (Thomas) Spotted Winged Fruit Bat
Cecadu Sayap Bertitik

Description: The smallest fruit bat in Malaysia (Figure 3.35). Upperparts blackish-brown with the fur on head darker, underparts greyish-brown. Wing membrane dark brown, flecked with small whitish spots, particularly on the joints of the digits. Pale spot on muzzle just in front of each eye. Nostrils elongated, almost tube-like and widely divergent. Five upper and lower cheek teeth with two pairs of upper incisors and one pair of lower incisors. Lacks an external tail. Closely resembles *Chironax melanocephalus* in structural features, from which it is distinguished by its smaller size, spotted wings and single pair of lower incisors.

FIGURE 3.35 *Balionycteris maculata* (Photo Juliana)

Measurements: (91 specimens) HB 53.0-62.0 mm, T nil, FA 38.7-44.0 mm, Tb 14.0-16.0 mm, E 9.0-11.0 mm, Wt 10.0-16.5 g. KWR: FA 38.4-43.8 mm (n = 25), Wt 11.0-15.5 g (n = 20). Mean FA of adult males at Kuala Lompat, KWR, significantly smaller (40.9 mm) than females (41.9 mm) (Hodgkison et al. 2003b). Mean aspect ratio 5.82, wing loading 9.51 Nm^{-2} (n = 20) (Hodgkison et al. 2004a).

Ecology: Primarily a forest species, found from lowland to hill and occasionally montane forests. It roosts in small groups in the crowns of palms and in clumps of ferns epiphytic on forest trees (Lekagul & McNeely 1988; Medway 1983). At Kuala Lompat, KWR, radio-tracking studies have identified five roost types: cavities in the root masses of epiphytic plant species (*Asplenium nidas* (Aspleniaceae) and *Hedychium longicornutum* (Zingiberaceae)); active arboreal nests of the ants *Crematogaster epinina*; abandoned arboreal termite *Bulbitermes* sp. nests (Figure 3.36); and the hollow base of a large detached branch (Hodgkison et al. 2003b). The roost itself is typically a smooth-surfaced bell-shaped cavity providing a semi-enclosed, sheltered space. The bats studied roosted in small harem groups of 1-14, one adult male and up to nine adult females and their dependent young, and it seems likely that the males excavate the roost cavity to attract females. At Kuala Lompat, both males and females forage within approximately 1 km of the roost (Hodgkison et al. 2003b), most commonly in the forest understorey

FIGURE 3.36 *Balionycteris maculata* in an abandoned termite nest in a sheltered boulder-cave (Photo Elder)

(Hodgkison et al. 2004a). Both harem and non-harem males regularly return to the roost at night, presumably to defend it. This species exploits plants showing a range of fruiting strategies at Kuala Lompat, from small understorey species in which slow sequential ripening provides a limited number of fruits throughout an extended (> 2 months) fruiting season to large canopy trees in which synchronous ripening of a large crop provides an abundance of fruit for less than two weeks (Hodgkison 2001). The diet at Kuala Lompat includes fruits of Annonaceae (*Cyathocalyx scortechinii, Polyalthia oblique, Pseuduvaria setosa var. major*), Ebenaceae (*Disopyros sumatrana*), Loganaceae (*Fagraea racemosa, Strychnos axilaris*), Melastomataceae (*Memyclon megacarpum, Pternandra echinata*), Moraceae (*Ficus fistulosa, Ficus globosa, Ficus scortechinii, Ficus sundaica*), Myrtaceae (*Eugenia griffithii, Eugenia* sp.), Rhizaphoraceae (*Pellacaclyx saccardianus*), Rubiaceae (*Diplospora malaccensis, Nauclea officinalis*), and Theaceae (*Adinandra sarosanthera*) (Hodgkison 2001).

Breeding: Thirty-two pregnant females were examined in February (8 specimens), March (7), April (4), May (5), June (3), September (3), and October (2). Females with dependent young were found in July (2). In the Cameron Highlands, all 12 females obtained and examined were pregnant in February and April (Lim 1967) suggesting a local seasonality in reproductive activities. Medway (1983) reported pregnant females in July, August and December. All pregnant females examined had only a single embryo. At Kuala Lompat, this species has a polyoestrus reproductive cycle, giving birth to up to two litters per year (one pup per litter, body mass c. 3.5 g, FA 19 mm), with approximately 135 days between successive births. Weaning occurs from approximately day 40 onwards, and adult size is reached after about six months. However, although lactating bats were captured throughout the year, the majority of females were lactating between May and November, during the fruiting season of the large-seeded non-pioneer food plants, and all but one pregnant female was captured between June and November (Hodgkison 2001).

KWR (lactating, pregnant): February/March (7, 1), April/May, (6, 0), June/July (12, 11), August/September (14, 10), October/November (10, 11), and December/January (4, 0).

IUCN: LR (lc).

Distribution KWR (Site, individuals, recaptures): Jenderak Selatan: 26, 0; Kuala Gandah: 12, 1; Kuala Lompat: 149, 138; Kuala Serloh: 21, 0; Lubuk Baung: 32, 0. Also captured at Lembah Klau. DWNP specimens from Kuala Lompat, Bukit Rengit and Sg. Chenderoh (Perlok). Captures at Kuala Lompat include those of Hodgkison (2001). Individuals captured by Kingston et al. (in press) were not banded, precluding detection of recaptures.

Distribution: Thailand, Peninsular Malaysia, Borneo, Sumatra, Durian, and Galang Islands (Riau Archipelago, Indonesia).

Chironax melanocephalus (Temminck) Black-capped Fruit Bat
Cecadu Kepala Hitam

FIGURE 3.37 *Chironax melanocephalus* (Photo Kingston)

Description: Upperparts dark brown to reddish, underparts pale brownish grey. The crown of the head is black with some individuals having a yellowish chin (Figure 3.37). Adults usually bear yellow-orange tufts on the sides of the neck, particularly older individuals. Tail is lacking. Four upper and five lower cheek teeth and two pairs of upper and lower incisors. Similar in appearance to *Balionycteris maculata* but distinguished by its comparatively larger size, presence of two pairs of lower incisors and absence of spots on the wings.

Measurements: (56 specimens) HB 55.0-72.0 mm, T nil, FA 44.0-48.5 mm, Tb 15.0-18.0 mm, E 11.0-15.0 mm, Wt 16.0-20.0 g. Mean aspect ratio 5.99, wing loading 11.14 Nm^{-2} (n = 16) (Hodgkison et al. 2004a).

Ecology: Common in lowland, hill and montane forests especially at higher elevations. It roosts gregariously in rock shelters and is also found in caves in forest. In the Cameron Highlands, it was found roosting on the underside of tree ferns in small groups of 2-8 individuals. At Kuala Lompat, KWR, two radio-tracked individuals (one male, one female) were both found to roost high in the forest sub-canopy (Hodgkison 2001), and the female was inferred to be roosting in a deep tree cavity of a large strangling fig. Based on capture records in nets stacked from the ground to 28 m at Kuala Lompat, this species forages at all heights below the canopy (Hodgkison et al. 2004a). It exploits plants showing a range of fruiting strategies, from small understorey plants in which slow sequential ripening of a medium to large crop provides fruits for an extended (> 2 months) fruiting season to large canopy trees in which synchronous ripening of a large crop provides an abundance of fruit for less than two weeks (Hodgkison 2001). Diet of this species at Kuala Lompat, includes fruits of Annonaceae (*Polyalthia oblique*), Ebenaceae (*Disopyros sumatrana*), Moraceae (*Ficus fistulosa, F. globosa, F. scortechinii*), Rhizaphoraceae (*Pellacaclyx saccardianus*), and Theaceae (*Adinandra sarosanthera*) (Hodgkison 2001).

Breeding: Eighteen females were found pregnant. February (10 specimens), March (2), April (1), June (1), and July (1). Three females with dependent young were found in February and March. Medway (1983) recorded most of the pregnant females in February and March, suggesting that breeding occurs primarily in the early part of the year.

IUCN: LR (lc).

Distribution KWR (Site, individuals, recaptures): Kuala Lompat: 48, 19. All but four captures at Kuala Lompat are those of Hodgkison (2001). Individuals captured by Kingston et al. (in press) were not banded, precluding detection of recaptures.

Distribution: Thailand, Peninsular Malaysia, Borneo, Sumatra, Java, Nias Islands, and Sulawesi.

Cynopterus brachyotis (Müller) Lesser Short-nosed Fruit Bat
Cecadu Pisang

FIGURE 3.38 *Cynopterus brachyotis* (Photo Juliana)

Description: Upperparts greyish brown to yellowish brown, often with dark orange around the shoulders and throat of adult males, more yellowish in females. Underparts paler (Figure 3.38). Young are usually greyish in colour. Ears and wing bones are edged in white in all three species of *Cynopterus* and all have four upper and five lower cheek teeth, two pairs of upper and lower incisors. Distinguished from *C. horsfieldii* by its smaller size, and lack of accessory cusps and ridges on the last lower premolar and first lower molar. Recent work suggests that across its geographic range *C. brachyotis* comprises up to six divergent mitochondrial lineages. The two lineages in Malaysia are broadly sympatric but appear to be ecologically and morphologically distinct, with one generally confined to primary and mature secondary forest (the Forest lineage - adult forearm length < 63 mm), and the other more broadly distributed in disturbed and agricultural habitats (Sunda lineage - FA > 64 mm) (Campbell et al. 2004) (Figure 3.39).

Measurements: (260 specimens, Sunda and Forest lineages combined) HB 72.0-90.0 mm, T 10.0-16.0 mm, FA 55.0-66.0 mm, Tb 21.0-25.0 mm, E 15.0-20.0 mm, Wt 28.0-40.0 g. Mean aspect ratio of Forest lineages at Kuala Lompat, KWR, 6.07, wing loading 11.88 Nm^{-2} (n = 28) (Hodgkison et al. 2004a).

Breeding: A total of 147 pregnant females found throughout the year were examined. The peak breeding period occurred in the first quarter (January-March), third quarter (July-Sept), fourth quarter (October-December) with lesser breeding activity in the second quarter (April-June). One young is born at a time, and carried by the female during the early part of its life. Medway (1983) and Lim (1970) reported pregnant females in all months with greater numbers from April to July in the lowland forests of Selangor.

FIGURE 3.39 *Cynopterus brachyotis* lineages: Forest (left) and Sunda (right). Forest bats tend to be smaller, with more slender skulls and elongated muzzles (Photo Campbell)

Ecology: *C. brachyotis* is the most common and abundant of the *Cynopterus* species. It is found in all types of habitat from lowland to submontane forests and is equally common in orchards, plantations and open country (although as detailed above, these observations may refer to two distinct lineages). They are commonly found in small harem groups in tent roosts. Tent roosts are constructed by chewing through the veins of a large leaf, so that part of the leaf collapses over and creates an enclosed space. The tent both hides the bats from visual predators and protects them from rain, and it is thought that the males make the tents to attract females. *C. brachyotis* in Malaysia mainly makes umbrella tents out of broad-leaf palms, but apical tents, conical tents and stem tents are also constructed from other plants (Tan et al. 1997). They also roost in unmodified plants, and occasionally caves and buildings. A single male radio-tracked at Kuala Lompat (KWR) was found roosting with two other individuals in a tent constructed from a furled banana leaf (Hodgkison 2001). They are important seed dispersers; their diet includes the fruits of at least 54 plant species, the leaves of 14 species, and the flower parts of a further four species (Tan et al. 1998). Based on capture records in stacked-net systems at Kuala Lompat, this species forages at all heights below the canopy (Hodgkison et al. 2004) where it exploits both asynchronously fruiting plants of the sub-canopy as well the large, synchronously produced crops of canopy trees. Diet of this species at Kuala Lompat includes fruits of Annonaceae (*Cyathocalyx scortechinii*), Elaeocarpaceae (*Elaeocarpus stipularis var. stipularis*), Melastomataceae (*Pternandra echinata*), Moraceae (*Ficus fistulosa, F. globosa,*

F. hispida, F. magneoleaefolia, F. scortechinii), Myrtaceae (*Eugenia chlorantha, Eugenia* sp.), Olacaceae (*Strombosia javanica*), Rhizaphoraceae (*Pellacaclyx saccardianus*), Rosaceae (*Prunus polystachya*), Rubiaceae (*Nauclea officinalis*), Sapotaceae (*Palaquium obovatum, Payena lucida*), and Theaceae (*Adinandra sarosanthera*) (Hodgkison 2001).

IUCN: LR (lc).

Distribution KWR (Site, individuals, recaptures): Kuala Gandah: 6, 0; Kuala Lompat: 208, 61; Kuala Serloh: 2, 0; Lubuk Baung: 1, 0. All but four captures at Kuala Lompat are those of Hodgkison (2001); individuals captured by Kingston et al. (in press) were not banded, precluding detection of recaptures. Also captured at Lembah Klau. DWNP specimens from Kuala Lompat, Bukit Rengit, Sg. Chenderoh (Perlok), Kuala Lompat, and Bukit Tapah (near Jerantut).

Distribution: Sri Lanka, India through SE Asia, Philippines, Nicobar and Andaman Islands, Borneo, Sumatra, Sulawesi, Magnole, Sanana, Sangihe Islands, and Talaud Islands.

Cynopterus horsfieldii Gray

Horsfield's Fruit Bat
Cecadu Pisang Besar

FIGURE 3.40 *Cynopterus horsfieldii* (Photo Kingston)

Description: Upperparts greyish-brown, underparts yellowish-brown with dark orange-red collar around the shoulder and throat in adult males (Figure 3.40). Ears and finger bones are edged white. Distinguished from *C. brachyotis* by greater size for almost all characters, and the presence of cusps and ridges on lower cheek teeth.

Measurements: (129 specimens) HB 85.0-120.0 mm, T 12.0-19.0 mm, FA 70.0-78.0 mm, Tb 25.0-31.0 mm, E 17.0-21.0 mm, Wt 43.0-65.0 g. Aspect ratio 5.84, wing loading 15.11 Nm^{-2} (n = 7) (Hodgkison et al. 2004a).

Ecology: This species is common and abundant and inhabits all habitat types at all elevations. It can be found from lowland, hill to submontane and montane forests including mangrove forest, orchards and plantations. It is highly gregarious when roosting in caves or rock shelters but tends to roost in smaller groups in forested areas or orchards. Based on capture records in stacked net systems at Kuala Lompat (KWR), this species forages at all heights below the canopy (Hodgkison et al. 2004a) and utilizes both asynchronously fruiting species of the midstorey (provided at least 50 percent of the canopy area is producing fruit at the time of visiting) as well as the large, synchronously-produced crops of canopy trees. Diet at Kuala Lompat includes fruits of Elaeocarpaceae (*Elaeocarpus stipularis* var. *stipularis*), Moraceae (*Ficus hispida*), and Sapotaceae (*Payena lucida*) (Hodgkison 2001).

Breeding: A total of 54 pregnant females were found throughout the year. Breeding activity was found to be higher in the first and second quarters and lower in the third and fourth quarters. Medway (1983) recorded pregnant females in every month in Selangor suggesting that breeding is aseasonal.

IUCN: LR (lc).

Distribution KWR (Site, individuals, recaptures): Kuala Lompat: 55, 4; Kuala Serloh: 1, 0. Captures at Kuala Lompat include those of Hodgkison (2001). Individuals captured by Kingston et al. (in press) were not banded, precluding detection of recaptures. DWNP specimens from Bukit Rengit and Sg. Chenderoh (Perlok).

Distribution: Thailand, Peninsular Malaysia, Borneo, Sumatra, and Lesser Sunda Islands.

Dyacopterus spadiceus (Thomas) — Dayak Fruit Bat
Cecadu Dayak

Description: Upperparts dark grey-brown to brown; unicoloured at lower back but fur with paler bases on shoulders and back of neck (Figure 3.41). Fur is short, but extends along the humerus to just above the elbow. Underparts pale buffy with a tinge of yellow. In some adults a neck gland stains the fur on the sides of the neck yellow-orange. The ears,

FIGURE 3.41 *Dyacopterus spadiceus* (Photo Kingston)

nostrils, and wings are brown, the claws are pale. The head is very broad and the muzzle short, the nostrils protrude approximately 20-30 degrees from the midline, and an internarial groove starts at base of nostrils and extends to upper lip (Figure 3.42). A short tail is present. Distinguished from all other fruit bats by having only three upper cheek teeth, which are extremely large and squarish and heavily cuspidate and ridged. It has five lower cheek teeth with two pairs of upper and lower incisors.

Measurements: (11 specimens) HB 80.0-117.0 mm, T 19.0-25.0 mm, FA 75.0-83.0 mm, Tb 28.0-29.0 mm, E 17.0-19.0 mm, Wt 55.0-110.5 g. Mean FA of adult males at Kuala Lompat, KWR, significantly large (77.4 mm) than females (75.6 mm) (Hodgkison 2001). Mean aspect ratio 6.25, wing loading 19.6 Nm^{-2} (n = 10) (Hodgkison et al. 2004a).

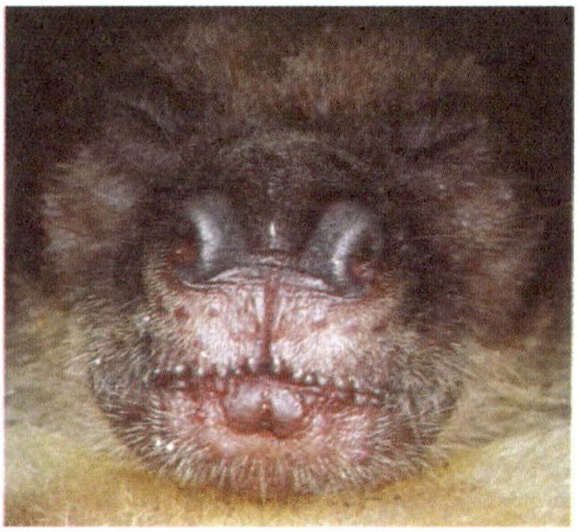

FIGURE 3.42 Groove bisecting upper lip. Note also buffy-yellow chest (Photo Kingston)

Breeding: Five females were found pregnant in January (1 specimen), March (2), October (1), and December (1). Lactation in adult males has been recorded in this species. 10 males captured at Kuala Lompat in 1992 and one in Perak had functional mammary glands from which small amounts of milk could be expressed (Francis et al. 1994).

Ecology: Mainly a forest inhabitant found in hill and montane forest. Of the 11 specimens examined, seven were from highland habitats. However, its presumed rarity in lowland habitats maybe a consequence of vertical stratification, as this species is likely to forage high in the canopy and subcanopy (Francis 1994, Hodgkison et al. 2004a), and is only captured at lower levels if nets are set by fruiting trees (T. Kingston, pers. obs.). At Kuala Lompat (KWR), this species forages in flocks at canopy trees bearing large crops and exhibiting a high degree of intra-crown crop maturation synchrony (Hodgkison 2001) and the diet includes fruits of Elaeocarpaceae (*Elaeocarpus stipularis var. stipularis*), Moraceae (*Ficus annulata, F. depressa*), and Rosaceae (*Prunus polystachya*) (Hodgkison 2001). It has been found roosting in small groups of 1-3 individuals in ferns, and at Kuala Lompat an individual male was radio-tracked to a tree cavity on the side of a large horizontal branch in the crown of a tall canopy tree (Hodgkison 2001).

IUCN: LR (nt).

Distribution KWR (Site, individuals, recaptures): Kuala Lompat: 33, 1. Captures at Kuala Lompat include those of Hodgkison (2001). Further individuals were captured by the MBCRU in a vertical net set by a fruiting tree near the Teris River at the forest boundary of Kuala Gandah. DWNP specimens from Kuala Lompat.

Distribution: NW Borneo, Luzon and Mindanao (Philippines), Peninsular Malaysia, and possibly S Thailand.

Penthetor lucasi (Dobson) — Lucas's Short-nosed Fruit Bat
Cecadu Hitam Pudar

Description: Upperparts dark grey-brown, underparts paler, buffy. Short tail. Ears have dark edges. Four upper and five lower cheek teeth, two pairs of upper incisors one pair of lower incisors. Similar in appearance to *Cynopterus brachyotis*, differing by the single pair of lower incisors and the dark-edged ears.

Measurements: (21 specimens) HB 78.0-103.0 mm, T 8.0-13.0 mm, FA 58.0-64.0 mm, Tb 23.0-29.0mm, E 14.0-17.0 mm, Wt 24.0-45.0 g.

Ecology: Inhabits forest of all elevations up to the summit of Gunung Brinchang, Pahang. It roosts mainly in caves, rock shelters and crevices in rock boulders in large colonies of more than 100 individuals. Occasional individuals were found roosting under palm trees in forests.

Breeding: Five females were found to be pregnant in September (4 specimens) and May (1). Medway (1983) recorded high numbers of pregnant females from Selangor in September and a few in June indicating seasonal reproductive activity, peaking in September.

IUCN: LR (lc)

Distribution KWR: A single individual was captured in a harp trap at Kuala Gandah.

Distribution: Peninsular Malaysia, Borneo, and Riau Archipelago.

Eonycteris spelaea (Dobson) Lesser Dawn Bat
Cecadu Gua

Description: Upperparts grey-brown to dark brown, underparts paler with neck and shoulders yellow in some individuals (Figure 3.43). The hair is generally quite sparse. Short external tail and no claw on the second digit of the wing. Both sexes have small, subcutaneous kidney-shaped glands on either side of the anus (function unknown). The muzzle is elongated and the skull generally adapted for drinking nectar, with a spout-shaped mandible to which tongue-extensor muscles are attached. Five upper and six lower cheek teeth with two pairs of upper and lower incisors. Distinguished from all other fruit bats by its lack of claw on the second digit of the wing.

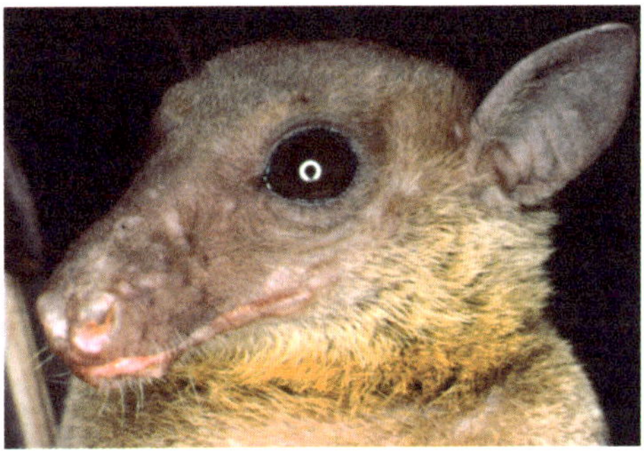

FIGURE 3.43 *Eonycteris spelaea* (Photo Kingston)

Measurements: (80 specimens) HB 85.0-110.0 mm, T 15.0-20.0 mm, FA 57.0-81.0 mm, Tb 26.0-33.0 mm, E 12.0-20.0 mm, Wt 41.0-72.0 g. Sexually dimorphic with males usually larger than females. Mean weight of adult males at Kuala Lompat, KWR, significantly greater (56.9 g) than females (47.7 g) (Hodgkison 2001). Mean aspect ratio 6.22, wing loading 18.19 Nm^{-2} (n = 11) (Hodgkison et al. 2004a).

Ecology: Primarily a cave dweller and can be found in limestone caves at all altitudes and on islands, forming large colonies that can sometimes exceed tens of thousands of individuals (Start 1974; Start & Marshall 1975; Lekagul and McNeely 1988). The diet consists mainly of nectar and pollen and as such this species is an important pollinator, particularly as individuals may travel up to 60 km from their roost in a night (Start 1974). Guano deposited by large colonies in the Dark Caves of Batu Caves (Selangor) included pollen grains of *Durio* spp., *Parkia* spp., *Artocarpus* spp., *Eugenia malaccensis* spp., *Duabonga grandiflora* spp., and a high percentage of *Sonneratia* spp. (Start & Marshall 1975). It is the primary pollinator of durian and petai, and may also be the sole pollinator for some species, e.g. *Oroxylum indicum* (Bignoniaceae) (Gould 1978a). Soft fruits are also included more rarely in the diet. At Kuala Lompat, KWR, it forages in flocks at canopy trees bearing large flower crops and exhibiting a high degree of intra-crown crop maturation synchrony (Hodgkison 2001), with the diet including flowers of Leguminosae (*Parkia javanica, P. speciosa*) and Sapotaceae (*Palaquium hispidum, P. obovatum*) (Hodgkison 2001).

Breeding: Sixteen females were found to be pregnant in January (10 specimens), March (2), and August (4). Females were found with dependent young in March (1), May (2), July (4), August (4), September (6), October (2), November (4), and December (5). Females are polyestrous and may become pregnant in the later stages of lactation (Beck & Lim 1973). Gestation is just over six months, and one young is more usual; twins are rare. The young are attached to the nipple for 4-6 weeks and are fully weaned by 3 months. Females reach sexual maturity after one year, males after two years.

IUCN: LR (lc).

Distribution KWR (Site, individuals, recaptures): Kuala Lompat: 182, 6. All but one capture at Kuala Lompat are those of Hodgkison (2001).

Distribution: India, Myanmar, Nepal, S China, Thailand, Laos, Peninsular Malaysia, Borneo, Sumatra, Java, Sumba, Timor and Sulawesi, Philippines, and Andaman Islands.

Macroglossus sobrinus K. Andersen Greater Long-nosed Fruit Bat
Cecadu Madu Besar

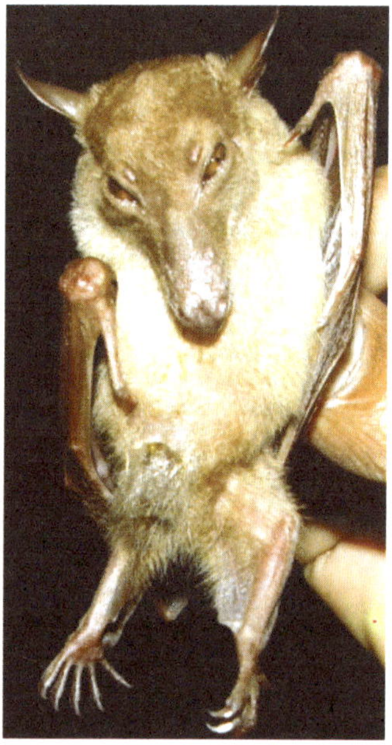

FIGURE 3.44 *Macroglossus sobrinus* (Photo Juliana)

Description: Uniformly light buffy brown (Figure 3.44). Flight membrane light brown. The muzzle is slender and elongated with a very long tongue that has a roughened brush-like tip. The upper incisors are small and sloped forward so that the long tongue may be used freely to reach nectar in deep-belled flowers. Tail either absent or very short. Median groove that extends from the upper lip to pass between the nostrils is vestigial, distinguishing it from *M. minimus* in which the groove is more apparent and is flanked by two smaller grooves near the upper lip.

Measurements: (90 specimens) HB 65.0-80.0 mm, T 0-5.0 mm, FA 41.0-48.0 mm, Tb 17.0-22.5 mm, E 13.0-18.0 mm, Wt 14.0-25.5 g.

Ecology: Inhabits forests of all elevations from lowland and hill to montane forests. Individuals were occasionally trapped from coastal mangroves. The diet consists of nectar and pollen, and it is frequently a key pollinator of wild banana plants *Musa* spp. and *Sonneratia* (Start & Marshall 1975).

Breeding: Fourteen females were found pregnant in January (2 specimens), February (3), March (1), May (1), June (3), July (1), and September (2) indicating non-seasonal breeding activity. Females with dependant young were found in August (1) and October (2).

IUCN: LR (lc).

Distribution KWR (Site, individuals, recaptures): Kuala Lompat: 3, 0; Kuala Serloh: 1, 0. Captures at Kuala Lompat are those of Hodgkison (2001). Also captured by the MBCRU in mist nets set near banana trees in the gardens of the Che Wong Orang Asli village at Kuala Gandah. DWNP specimens from Bukit Rengit.

Distribution: NE India, Myanmar, C and S Thailand, Peninsular Malaysia, S Laos, Vietnam, Sumatra, Java, Bali, Sipora, Siberut, Mentawai Islands (Indonesia), and Borneo.

Megaerops ecaudatus (Temminck) Temmink's Tailless Fruit Bat
Cecadu Tiada Ekor

Description: Upperparts pale greyish-brown to yellowish uniformly, underparts paler and greyer. Ears are pale brown and translucent. Muzzle is short and broad, with the nostrils distinctly projecting, almost tubular. Tail lacking. Two pairs of upper incisors and only one pair of lower incisors. Distinguished from *M. wetmorei* by larger size and absence of white shoulder tufts.

Measurements: (40 specimens) HB 65.0-84.0 mm, T nil, FA 50.0-58.0 mm, Tb 19.0-23.0 mm, E 13.0-18.0 mm, Wt 24.0-40.0 g. Mean FA of adult males at Kuala Lompat, KWR significantly smaller (52.3 mm) than females (54.6 mm) (Hodgkison 2001).

Ecology: Primarily a forest inhabitant ranging from lowland and hill to montane forests. Hodgkison et al. (2004a) found it foraging at all heights below the canopy, although Francis (1994) found it to be more common in the subcanopy than at ground level. Little is known of the habits of this genus, although at Kuala Lompat a single male was radio-tracked to a roosting position high in the canopy within 50 m of a fruiting tree at which it had been foraging. This species may be nomadic, utilizing transient roost sites to exploit large, ephemeral fruit crops (Hodgkison 2001). At Kuala Lompat, it exploits canopy trees bearing large crops and exhibiting a high degree of intra-crown crop maturation synchrony (Hodgkison 2001) and the diet includes fruits of Elaeocarpaceae (*Elaeocarpus stipularis* var. *stipularis*), Moraceae (*Ficus globosa, F. magneoleaefolia*), Myrtaceae (*Eugenia chlorantha*), Olacaceae (*Strombosia javanica*), Rhizaphoraceae (*Pellacaclyx saccardianus*), Rosaceae (*Prunus polystachya*), and Sapotaceae (*Palaquium obovatum*) (Hodgkison 2001).

Breeding: Sixteen females were found to be pregnant in February (10 specimens), May (5) and June (1). Lim (1973) reported most pregnant females in the month of February. Medway (1983) recorded pregnant females in February mostly from Cameron Highlands, with pregnancies elsewhere in February and March and females with dependent young in November.

IUCN: LR (lc).

Distribution KWR (Site, individuals, recaptures): Kuala Lompat: 50, 0. All but three captures are those of Hodgkison (2001). DWNP specimens from Bukit Rengit.

Distribution: Thailand, possibly Vietnam, Peninsular Malaysia, Borneo, and Sumatra.

Megaerops wetmorei Taylor — White-collared Fruit Bat
Cecadu Bahu Putih

Description: Similar in colouration to *M. ecaudatus*, but with large white tufts on the shoulders and side of neck forming a collar that extends onto the back (lacking in some individuals). All other characters are identical to *M. ecaudatus*, from which it is further distinguished by its smaller size.

Measurements: (4 specimens) HB 58.0-68.0 mm, T nil, FA 45.0-50.0 mm, Tb 12.0-13.0 mm, E 11.0-17.0 mm, Wt 23.0-26.0 g.

Ecology: Reported as a new record for Peninsular Malaysia by Francis (1989) at Pasoh Forest Reserve, Negri Sembilan. Little is known of its ecology with the exception that it was netted in forested areas, and at KWR was apparently common in nets set in the subcanopy between July and September 1992 (Francis 1994). However, Hodgkison (2001) captured only three individuals on a single occasion when nets were set at a food tree (*Palaquium obovatum* (Sapotaceae)), despite two 12-month field seasons between May 1997 and November 1999.

Breeding: A single pregnant female was found in August.

IUCN: LR (lc).

Distribution KWR (Site, individuals, recaptures): Kuala Lompat: 15, 0 (Francis 1994; Hodgkison 2001). DWNP specimen from Kuala Lompat.

Distribution: Peninsular Malaysia, Borneo, Sumatra, and Minadao Island (Philippines).

Rousettus amplexicaudatus (E. Geoffroy) Geoffroy's Rousette Bat
Cecadu Besar

Description: Upperparts are uniform dull greyish-brown, underparts grey to brown. Sparsely furred. The flight membrane is dark brown. It has a short tail, and two pairs of upper and lower incisors, five upper and six lower cheek teeth. Similar to *Eonycteris spelaea*, differs in the presence of a claw on the second digit and by having a shorter and more robust muzzle.

Measurements: (15 specimens) HB 105.0-120.0 mm, T 18.0-20.0 mm, FA 78.0-95.0 mm, Tb 32.0-38.0 mm, E 17.0-20.0 mm, Wt 63.0-93.5 g. Mean aspect ratio 6.34, wing loading 17.80 Nm^{-2} (n = 20) (Hodgkison et al. 2004a).

Ecology: Primarily a cave dweller, but will also roost in the crevices of large rock boulders. Found in forested and agricultural areas at all altitudes from lowland, to montane forest. In primary forest, rarely caught below the canopy (Hodgkison et al. 2004a). When in flight it produces a distinctive clicking sound through the movement of the tongue against the palate, a basic form of echolocation restricted to this megachiropteran genus (Novick 1958). Very little is known of its natural diet. However, Medway (1983) reported that captive specimens thrived on mixed fruits, milk and sweetened solution of Complan. At Kuala Lompat, KWR, it forages at canopy trees bearing large crops and exhibiting a high degree of intra-crown crop maturation synchrony, and the diet includes fruits of Elaeocarpaceae (*Elaeocarpus stipularis* var. *stipularis*) (Hodgkison 2001).

Breeding: Four females were found to be pregnant in January (1 specimen) and March (3). In the Philippines, reproduction is synchronous and seasonal, and older females may breed twice a year (Heideman & Utzurrum 2003).

IUCN: LR (lc).

Distribution KWR: Nine individuals captured at Kuala Lompat (Francis 1994; Hodgkison 2001).

Distribution: Cambodia, Thailand, Laos, Peninsular Malaysia through Indonesia, Java, Bali, Philippines, New Guinea, Bismarck Archipelago and Solomon Islands.

Suborder Microchiroptera

In Peninsular Malaysia the Microchiroptera includes seven families comprising 26 genera and approximately 109 species. Representatives of each family are found at KWR, and to date at least 58 species have been recorded in the reserve. All Microchiroptera echolocate and the majority of species in the Old World are insectivorous, with a few species taking small vertebrate prey.

Family Emballonuridae - Sheath-tailed Bats

The family is represented by four species in three genera in Peninsular Malaysia, two species have been reported for KWR. The diagnostic character for the family is the tail which protrudes dorsally from the tail membrane within a membranous sheath. There is no noseleaf, the eyes are large, and the tragus is short and club- or mushroom-shaped.

Emballonura monticola Temminck — Lesser Sheath-tailed Bat
Kelawar Teng-teng Ceteng

Description: This species is recognised by its very small size and dark colouration. Upperparts dark brown to chestnut-brown with paler bases, the fur is long (Figure 3.45). Underparts are paler buffy-brown. The wings are black, and the 1st phalanx of 3rd finger folds upwards to lie against dorsal side of wing when at rest (as in *Taphozous*). The sheathed tail emerges from the dorsal side of the tail membrane approximately

FIGURE 3.45 *Emballonura monticola* (Photo Elder)

half of the way along its length, and is shorter than the total membrane length. The muzzle is without fur and the skin is brown. The ears are brown with a small, mushroom-shaped tragus. The eyes are large.

Measurements: (32 specimens) HB 40.0-47.0 mm, T 11.0-14.0 mm, FA 43.0-47.0 mm, Tb 8.0-10.0 mm, E 10.0-13.0 mm, Wt 5.0-7.0 g. KWR: FA 38.9-46.4 mm (n = 41), Wt 4.0-8.5 g (n = 41).

Echolocation: Dominated by a CF component between 48 and 51 kHz, the signals of this species are highly distinctive, starting with a slight upsweep before the CF component and ending in a terminal downsweep. The calls are superficially rather like those of the Rhinolophidae but are generally shorter (6-8 ms) and the CF component encompasses a slightly broader band of frequencies, giving a 'humped' appearance to spectograms and a broader peak in the power spectra. It is the second harmonic that is emitted most strongly, with the fundamental often apparent but greatly attenuated. Other harmonics are also expressed, particularly when flying low or near vegetation. During the feeding buzz, the frequency range is only slightly enlarged, and the fundamental may become more pronounced (Heller 1989).

Ecology: All the specimens were caught in primary forest ranging from lowland and hill to montane forest up to 1,800 m. They roost in overhanging dead logs, under buttresses of fallen trees, crevices of rocks and in the lighter areas of cave and boulder systems. They roost gregariously in small groups of 2-15 individuals. They have a distinctive roosting posture, with the forearm propped against the side of the roost and the head facing dorsally (Figure 3.46). In the forest they are often found near streams. They forage in small gaps in the forest interior and at the forest edge, over streams and in disturbed forest, and are often among the first species observed foraging.

FIGURE 3.46 *Emballonura monticola* roosting in a cave showing distinctive roosting posture (Photo Elder)

Breeding: Five out of the nine females were found to be pregnant with a single embryo each in October (2 specimens), December (2), and January (1). Medway (1983) reported pregnant females in February, March, October, and November of specimens examined in Selangor. Lactating females in Gua Kota Gelanggi (Jerantut, Pahang) in January. KWR: Lactating females in May (2) and July (1), one pregnant in September.

IUCN: LR (lc).

Distribution KWR (Site, individuals, recaptures): Jenderak Selatan: 1, 0; Kuala Gandah: 8, 0; Kuala Lompat: 7, 0; Kuala Serloh: 13, 0; Lubuk Baung: 3, 0. This species does not forage in the forest understorey and is generally only caught in harp traps set near to a roost, or near small clearings, and accounts < 1% of individuals at all sites. DWNP specimens from Bukit Rengit.

Distribution: Thailand to Peninsular Malaysia, Borneo, Sumatra, Riau Arch., Banka, Billiton, Engano, Babi Islands, Batu Islands, Niah Islands, Mentawi Islands, Java, and Sulawesi.

Taphozous melanopogon Temminck — Black-bearded Tomb Bat
Kelawar Dagu Hitam

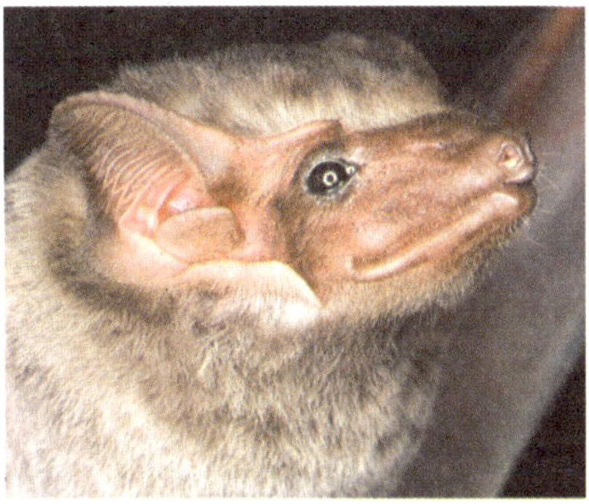

FIGURE 3.47 *Taphozous melanopogon* (Photo Kingston)

FIGURE 3.48 Ventral view of left wrist to show radio-metacarpal pouch (Photo Kingston)

Description: Upperparts bicoloured with pale brown to buffy brown tips with white bases (Figure 3.47). Underparts are paler with light grey-brown tips and white bases. Chin pouch absent, but males usually have a black beard, the hairs of which are larger and specialized for holding and dispersing glandular products that empty into the beard via a series of pores, although this may not be present in younger animals. Females have short fur under the chin. There is a radio-metacarpal pouch present (Figure 3.48). Wings pale whitish-brown and translucent, especially distally, and appear whitish in flight. First phalanx of third finger folds upwards to lie against dorsal side of wing when at rest. The tail is short and projects dorsally from the tail membrane within a sheath of skin (Figure 3.49). Tail membrane light brown, the calcar is large and the legs and feet covered with short hairs. The muzzle is without fur, the skin is a pinkish brown. The ears are the same colour with a short, broad, trapezoid tragus. The lower margin of the ear extends to chin, just below corner of the mouth, and the ear is heavily concertinaed along posterior margin (Figure 3.47). The eyes are large. Differs from *Saccolaimus saccolaimus* by the presence of wing pouch and from *Taphozous longimanus* by lack of a chin pouch.

Measurements: (81 adult specimens) HB 70.0-98.0 mm, T 22.0-29.0 mm, FA 62.0-68.0 mm, Tb 24.0-27.0 mm, E 18.0-24.0 mm, Wt 22.0-35.0 g.

Echolocation: Calls are long, narrowband and multiharmonic. Typically 6-14 ms (rarely up to 17 ms), with the dominant 2nd harmonic starting at 26-30 kHz and sweeping down to 24-26 kHz (average frequency drop 2 kHz) (Heller 1989), with a peak frequency averaging 27 kHz (T. Wood unpub. data).

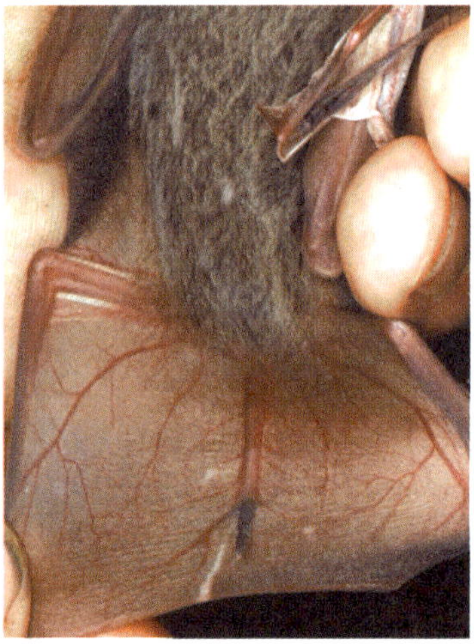

FIGURE 3.49 Dorsal view of tail of *T. melanopogon*, showing sheath and pale, translucent tail membrane (Photo Kingston)

Ecology: The specimens were collected in lowland and hill forest, caves and buildings in urban areas. They are highly gregarious and can be found roosting at the entrance of limestone caves in large colonies (or further into caves if there is some light reaching them), and in smaller groups in crevices and caves created by boulders (3-6 bats). In the forest they have been found to roost in holes of dead tree trunks and old rubber trees in plantations. They may forage in small groups; T. Kingston observed small groups (< 7 individuals) assembling at dusk on the side of a boulder cave and flying off together after a single bat had emitted an audible contact call. Based on wing morphology and visual observations they are presumed to forage high above the canopy or in open spaces, so they are rarely captured at ground level. Feed on termite swarms (Gould 1978b), and are parasitized by *Eoctenes intermedius* (Hemiptera: Polyctenidae).

Breeding: Of the 28 females examined 7 were found to be pregnant with a single embryo each in August (2 specimens), September (1) and December (4). Medway (1983) reported that these bats breed seasonally in Batu Caves, Selangor, with the highest proportion of pregnancies in January.

IUCN: LR (lc).

Distribution KWR: A single individual was netted at Kuala Lompat by Zubaid (1993).

Distribution: Sri Lanka, India, Myanmar, Thailand, Laos, Cambodia, Vietnam, S China, Peninsular Malaysia and adjacent islands, Borneo, Lesser Sunda Islands, Sumatra, Java, Lombok, Sumbawa, Moyo, Alor, Timor, Kei Islands, and Sulawesi.

Family Nycteridae - Slit-faced Bats

This family is represented by a single genus with only one species, *Nycteris tragata*, in Peninsular Malaysia.

Nycteris tragata (K. Andersen)

Malayan Slit-faced Bat
Kelawar Muka Lekok

FIGURE 3.50 *Nycteris tragata* (Photo Juliana)

Description: Very long, brown ears separated at the base, with a short, rounded tragus deep in the ear that curves forward (Figure 3.50). The face has a deep groove in the middle, extending from the nostrils to a point level with the eyes, with folds of skin either side forming leaflets. The tail is as long as the head and body and completely enclosed within the interfemoral membrane with a T-shaped or Y-shaped cartilaginous tip that supports the free edge of the membrane in conjunction with a long (< 20 mm) calcar (Figure 3.51). The fur is long and fluffy and is reddish-brown to light brown with paler bases. Undersides are slightly paler. Wing membranes are brown; fingers pinkish-brown. The forearm is thickly furred from the base to approximately half its length, as is the humerus. Wing is very broad and short, with an extensive propatagium, and the membrane between the 1st and 2nd finger is also well developed and supported by the long thumb. The eyes are small.

Measurements: (30 specimens) HB 50.0-65.0 mm, T 65.0-80.0 mm, FA 47.0-63.0 mm, Tb 28.0-32.0 mm, E 26.0-32.0 mm, Wt 14.0-19.0 g. KWR:

FA 47.6-54.9 mm (n = 74), Wt 12.5-22.5 g (n = 72).

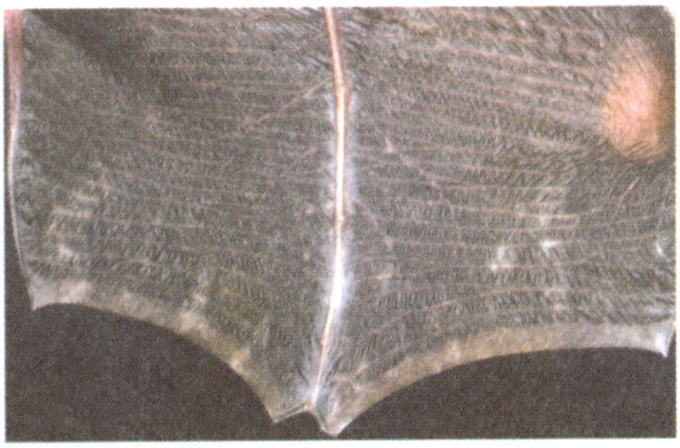

FIGURE 3.51 Tail of *Nycteris tragata* extending to end of tail membrane where it finishes in Y- or T- shaped cartilage (Photo Kingston)

Echolocation: Low intensity, short duration (2-3 ms) multiharmonic FM sweep comprising upto 3-4 harmonic components (T. Kingston, unpub. data).

Ecology: Primarily a forest species. The specimens were all captured in lowland, hill and montane forest. They roost in small groups of 2-8 individuals in tree holes, hollows in fallen trees (Figures 3.52 and 3.53) and similar man-made hollows such as culverts, as well as in crevices of large boulders and deep in the caverns of limestone caves. Thought to hunt for prey using passive listening - large ears enable them to hear the rustling of prey and low wing-loading enables them to lift off from the ground with relatively large prey items.

FIGURE 3.52 *Nycteris tragata* roost at Kuala Lompat, KWR (Photo Struebig)

FIGURE 3.53 Roosting *Nycteris tragata* (Photo Juliana)

Breeding: Of the 12 females examined, 5 were found pregnant with a single embryo each in February (1 specimen), April (1), May (1) and November (2). Medway (1983) reported pregnant females in March and lactating females in February, July and November. KWR (lactating, pregnant): February (1, 2), April (1, 0), June

(1, 0), July (2, 0), August (1, 0), and September (0, 1).

IUCN: LR (lc).

Distribution KWR (Site, individuals, recaptures): Jenderak Selatan: 17, 4; Kuala Gandah: 11, 2; Kuala Lompat: 8, 2; Kuala Serloh: 6, 0; Lubuk Baung: 16, 1. A relatively rare bat accounting for < 1% of captured individuals at all sites. Also captured at Lembah Klau. DWNP specimens from Bukit Rengit.

Distribution: Myanmar, Thailand, Peninsular Malaysia, Java, Sumatra, and Borneo.

Family Megadermatidae - False Vampire Bats

This family is represented by a single genus with two species in Peninsular Malaysia, of which just one has been recorded at KWR. They are characterised by having very large round ears that are joined at their bases over the top of the head, and a long bifid tragus. The noseleaf, another distinctive character, is a long dorsal lobe with a stiffened central ridge supporting flaps on both sides. The interfemoral membrane is large but the tail is not visible externally.

Megaderma spasma (Linnaeus) — Lesser False Vampire
Kelawar Telinga Lebar

Description: Ears are very large and rounded and joined at the bases over the top of the head (Figure 3.54). A long bifid tragus is present (Figure 3.55). The noseleaf is a long dorsal lobe with a stiffened central ridge supporting flaps on both sides. In this species the intermediate leaf is broad, chordate and the posterior is broadly elliptical, slightly rounded above (Figure 3.56). The interfemoral membrane is large but the tail is not visible externally. The fur is long, fluffy and is pale grey to dull brown in adults. Juveniles are uniformly grey in colour.

Measurements: (29 specimens) HB 65.0-82.0 mm, T nil, FA 56.0-62.0 mm, Tb 31.0-34.0 mm, E 30.0-36.0 mm, Wt 20.0-31.0 g. KWR: FA 53.1-63.6 mm (n = 34), Wt 20.0-31.0 g. KWR: FA 53.1-63.6 mm (n = 34), Wt 18.0-34.0 g (n = 33).

FIGURE 3.54 *Megaderma spasma* (Photo Wood)

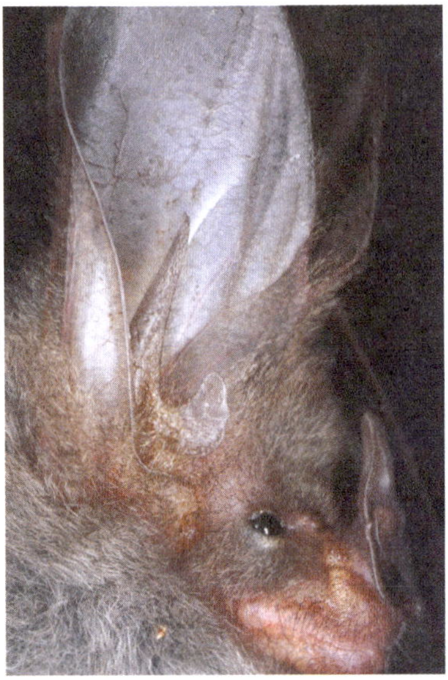

FIGURE 3.55 Side view of *Megaderma spasma* to show bifurcate (bifid) tragus (Photo Kingston)

Echolocation: Calls much like those of *Nycteris tragata*: low intensity, short duration, multi-harmonic FM sweeps.

Ecology: Primarily a forest inhabitant but also found in caves (Figure 3.57) and occasionally in large tree hollows, culverts, tunnels, crevices of rock-boulders, and abandoned outbuildings. They are gregarious and roost in small groups of 2-5 individuals. Diet includes large insects like grasshoppers, cockroaches, dung beetles and moths, and occasionally small vertebrates such as frogs and mice. *M. spasma* is the only known host of the polyctenid parasite *Eoctenes spasmae* which spends its entire life on the bat, most commonly on the back (Marshall 1982).

FIGURE 3.56 Noseleaf of *M. spasma* (Photo Kingston)

Breeding: Of the 12 females examined 5 were found pregnant with a single embryo each. January (1 specimen), April (1), May (2) and October (1). Medway (1983) reported pregnant females in Selangor in February, March, April, and August. KWR: two females captured lactating in May, one in June.

FIGURE 3.57 Small colony of *Megaderma spasma* in a cave roost (Photo Hall)

IUCN: LR (lc).

Distribution KWR (Site, individuals, recaptures): Jenderak Selatan: 7, 0; Kuala Gandah: 5, 0; Kuala Lompat: 11, 1; Kuala Serloh: 2, 1; Lubuk Baung: 3, 1. A relatively rare bat accounting for < 1% of captured individuals at all sites. DWNP specimens from Bukit Rengit.

Distribution: Sri Lanka and India through SE Asia to Lesser Sundas, the Philippines and Molucca Islands, and various adjacent islands.

Family Rhinolophidae - Horseshoe Bats

The family comprises a single genus, *Rhinolophus* with at least 18 species described for Peninsular Malaysia, of which nine are found in KWR. They are small to medium-sized bats characterised by a complex noseleaf (Figure 3.12) comprising three parts: a horseshoe-shaped, flat anterior noseleaf that surrounds the nostrils and covers some part of the muzzle; an upstanding central projection, the sella, that arises medially and may bear lateral processes; and a posterior noseleaf which is lancet-shaped and arises behind the sella. The sella is joined to the posterior noseleaf by the connecting process, and the shape of the sella and connecting process differ diagnostically among species. There is no tragus but the large, prominent ears have an antitragus. The eyes are small and often partially hidden by the noseleaf. The tail is rather long and is enclosed within the interfemoral membrane.

Rhinolophus luctus Temminck

Woolly Horseshoe Bat
Kelawar Ladam Berbulu

Description: This is the largest of the horseshoe bats found in Malaysia (Figure 3.58). The hairs on the upperparts are fairly long (at least 1 cm) and woolly with the tips of the longer hairs either pale brown or grey, giving a frosted appearance. The underparts are dark grey to dark brown. The noseleaf is dull black and the anterior leaf is large, projecting over the muzzle and deeply grooved in the centre. The sella has a lappet (Figures 3.59 and 3.12) on each side. The lancet is long and slightly blunt on the tip. The ears are long and pointed with the outer margin concave below the tip. Distinguished from all other horseshoe bats by large size.

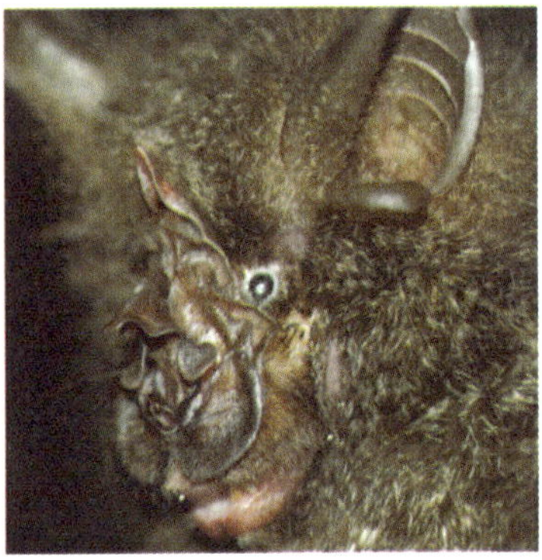

FIGURE 3.58 *Rhinolophus luctus* (Photo Juliana)

FIGURE 3.59 Noseleaf of *Rhinolophus luctus* (Photo Juliana)

Measurements: (16 specimens) HB 70.0-85.0 mm, T 40.0-52.0 mm, FA 62.0-69.0 mm, Tb 30.0-36.0 mm, E 30.0-35.0 mm, Wt 30.0-40.9 g. KWR: FA 60.2-68.3 mm, Wt 25.5-39.0 g (n = 15).

Echolocation: CF 40-42 kHz (Kingston et al. 2000a).

Ecology: Found in primary forests at all elevations, as well as some secondary forests. It roosts singly or in pairs and not in colonies like many other *Rhinolophus*. Roosting sites include caves, rock shelters, hollow trees, fallen tree hollows, or under thick bark at subcanopy level. Has been observed perch-hunting.

Breeding: Of seven females examined, four were found pregnant with a single embryo each in January (1 specimen), April (1), June (1) and August (1). A pregnant female at KWR was recorded in August, 2 lactating females in October and a juvenile in June and in February. May breed all year round.

IUCN: LR (lc).

Distribution KWR (Site, individuals, recaptures): Jenderak Selatan: 4, 0; Kuala Gandah: 3, 1; Kuala Lompat: 4, 0; Kuala Serloh: 7, 0; Lubuk Baung: 1, 0. Rarely captured, accounting for < 1% of individuals at all sites. DWNP specimens from Bukit Rengit.

Distribution: India, Nepal, Myanmar, Sri Lanka, S China, Taiwan, Vietnam, Cambodia, Laos, Thailand, Peninsular Malaysia, Borneo, Sumatra, Java, and Bali.

Rhinolophus trifoliatus Temminck — Trefoil Horseshoe Bat
Kelawar Ladam Muka Kuning

Description: Upperparts pale buffy-grey to brown, underparts paler. Noseleaf is pale yellow as are the elbows, knees and ears, particularly in older animals (Figure 3.60). The wing membrane is a tan brown. The noseleaf has lateral lappets at the base of the sella similar to *R. luctus* (Figure 3.61). Differs from *R. luctus* by colour and smaller size, and from *R. sedulus* by colour and larger size.

FIGURE 3.60 *Rhinolophus trifoliatus* (Photo Kingston)

Measurements: (119 specimens) HB 51.0-64.0 mm, T 30.0-44.0 mm, FA 40.0-57.0 mm, Tb 23.0-27.5 mm, E 24.0-27.0 mm, Wt 14.0-18.0 g. KWR: FA 44.8-56.1 mm, Wt 8.0-20.0 g (n = 436).

Echolocation: CF 53 kHz (Kingston et al. 2000a).

Ecology: A common species that

inhabits primary and secondary forests at all elevations, and mangrove forest. It is often caught in the understorey. In KWR roosting ecology was studied by radio-tracking 12 females and 20 males. All individuals were found roosting alone (except females with pups) in understorey foliage, often under leaves of palms and rattan as well as small trees, and generally less than 3 m above the ground. Individuals frequently switched roosts, using from two to eight roosts during the life of the transmitter (up to eight days) from day to day, although it is not certain whether this was a consequence of the disturbance caused by the study, as most roosting sites are relatively exposed and the bat was occasionally flushed from its roost. Typically, new roosts were selected < 100 m from the original roost site, and old roosts were occasionally re-used after an interval of a few days (C. Fletcher unpub. data). Medway (1983) also recorded it from caves. It is a perch hunter that scans for flying insect prey from a branch in the understorey, with a clear area below. Radio-tracking studies at Lubuk Baung indicate that this species forages within a relatively small distance (< 150 m) of the roost, and this is further supported by the small average recapture distances recorded over three years at that site (65 m - 12 males; 62 m - 12 females).

FIGURE 3.61 Noseleaf of *Rhinolophus trifolatus (Photo Kingston)*

Breeding: Of 51 females examined, 18 were found pregnant with a single embryo each, with 2 specimens carrying twin embryos. Pregnant females were recorded in January (4 specimens), March (2), April (2), May (2), June (1), August (1), September (4), and November (2). Medway (1983) collected pregnant females in May, June, September through November. Based on Medway's record and the present findings, it appears this species breed all year round, but at KWR there was a peak in breeding activity in the first half of the year with 20/24 pregnancies recorded between February and March, and 52/60 lactating females captured between April and July. Nearly half of the lactating females were recorded in May.

IUCN: LR (lc).

Distribution KWR (Site, individuals, recaptures): Jenderak Selatan: 139, 15; Kuala Gandah: 123, 34; Kuala Lompat: 110, 27; Kuala Serloh: 87, 18; Lubuk Baung: 93, 11. A relatively common species at all sites where it accounts for 4-6% of all individuals captured at each site. Also captured at Lembah Klau. DWNP specimens from Bukit Rengit and Sg. Chenderoh (Perlok).

Distribution: NE India, Myanmar, SW Thailand, Peninsular Malaysia, Borneo, Sumatra, Riau Arch., Banguey Island, Java, Banka Island, and Nias Island.

Rhinolophus sedulus Andersen

Lesser Woolly Horseshoe Bat
Kelawar Ladam Bulu Halus

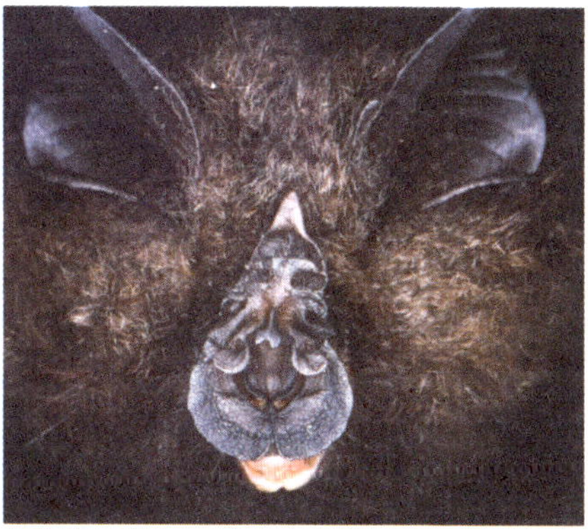

FIGURE 3.62 *Rhinolophus sedulus* (Photo Kingston)

Description: Colour of fur similar to *R. luctus*, although sometimes a darker brown to dark grey, sometimes with greyish tips. Underside also brown. The fur is long and fluffy. Noseleaf and ears dark brown or black. The noseleaf has lateral lappets at base of the sella (Figures 3.62). Differs from *R. luctus* by being very much smaller in size and from *R. trifoliatus* by colour and smaller size.

Echolocation: CF 67 kHz (Kingston et al. 2000a).

Measurements: (7 specimens) HB 47.0-51.0 mm, T 19.0-30.0 mm, FA 39.0-43.0 mm, Tb 19.0-20.5 mm, E 17.0-21.0 mm, Wt 5.6-10.2 g. KWR: FA 37.0-48.0 mm, Wt 6.0-11.5 g (n =119).

Ecology: Mainly a lowland primary forest species. Medway (1983) reported it roosting in caves and also netted in forest far from caves, and it sometimes utilizes man-made structures such as culverts (Heller & Volleth 1989). Radio-tracking of ten individuals at KWR (C. Fletcher, T. Kingston unpub. data) has found them roosting in pairs or singly in fallen tree hollows, the cavities formed at the base of large fallen trees, and on three occasions in foliage in the understorey. Up to five roosts were used during the life-span of the transmitter (up to eight days), but most individuals were faithful to one or two roosts unless disturbed. There is some suggestion that the species may be monogamous (Heller et al. 1993).

Breeding: Of four females examined, one was found pregnant in May. At KWR, lactating females were found in May (6), June (2), July (1) September (1), and October (1).

IUCN: LR (lc).

Distribution KWR (Site, individuals, recaptures): Jenderak Selatan: 35, 11; Kuala Gandah: 59, 20; Kuala Lompat: 11, 2; Kuala Serloh: 26, 2; Lubuk Baung: 26, 3. Although present in low numbers at all sites, the contribution to the total captures of individuals varied from as low as 0.7% at Kuala Lompat to over 3% at Kuala Gandah. Recapture rates were also noticeably higher at Jenderak Selatan and Kuala Gandah, exceeding 30% in both cases. DWNP specimens from Bukit Rengit and Kuala Lompat.

Distribution: Peninsular Malaysia and Borneo.

Rhinolophus macrotis Blyth — Big-eared Horseshoe Bat
Kelawar Ladam Telinga Panjang

Description: Upperparts light brown uniformly, underparts buffy. The ears are large. The noseleaf is hairy and highly distinctive; the sella lacks lateral lappets but is broad and set in a cup-like expansion of the nostril margins, and the connecting process is notched where it meets the sella (Figure 3.63). The anterior noseleaf is large, covering the upper lip but the posterior noseleaf is comparatively short, blunt at the apex. Distinguished from all other *Rhinolophus* species by the distinctive formation of the expansion of the nostril margins.

Echolocation: CF 48 kHz (Kingston et al. 2000a).

Measurements: (16 specimens) HB 45.0-56.0 mm, T 22.0-25.0 mm, FA 42.0-50.0 mm, Tb 17.0-23.0 mm, E 23.0-26.0 mm, Wt 7.0-13.5 g. KWR:

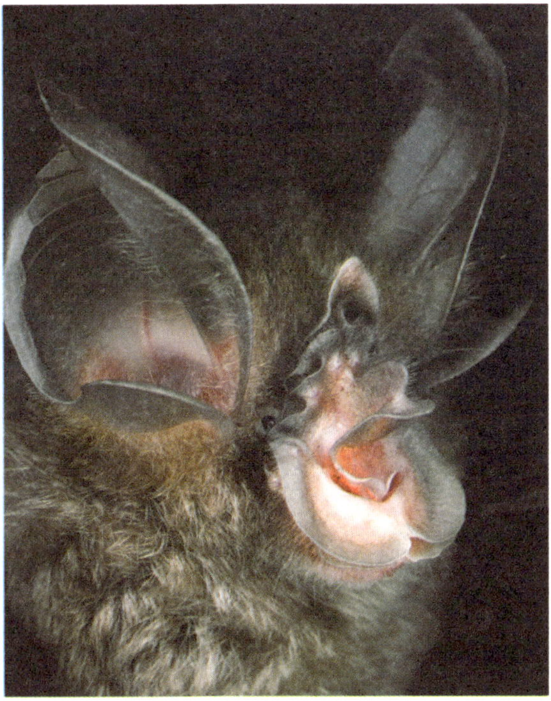

FIGURE 3.63 *Rhinolophus macrotis* (Photo Kingston)

FA 45.5-46.5 mm, Wt 7.5 g (n = 2).

Ecology: Little is known. Medway (1983) reported specimens collected on the eastern slopes of Gunung Benom 200-1000 m in Pahang and also at Pulau Langkawi, Kedah. Other specimens have been netted in hill forest of about 300 metres in elevation. Individuals in KWR captured in harp traps in lowland forest.

Breeding: Of the 14 females examined, 11 were found pregnant in March with a single foetus each. Medway (1983) recorded pregnant females in February-March.

IUCN: LR (lc).

Distribution KWR: A single individual was captured at Kuala Gandah, in a harp trap set just inside the forest (not part of the standardised grid study). Two individuals were captured at Kuala Lompat between 1995 and 1997 (Kingston et al. 2003a), and a fourth at Kuala Serloh in February 2005. DWNP specimens from Sg. Chenderoh (Perlok). Medway (1983) reported specimens collected on the eastern slopes of Gunung Benom.

Distribution: N India to S China, Laos, Vietnam, Peninsular Malaysia, Sumatra, and Philippines.

Rhinolophus stheno K Andersen — Lesser Brown Horseshoe Bat
Kelawar Ladam Bukit

Description: Upperparts dark brown to reddish brown or orange (from bleaching in some caves). Underparts are uncoloured either reddish or greyish brown with markings contrasting with the upperparts. The noseleaf is small and the lancet low and bluntly pointed (Figure 3.64). The connecting process is rounded (Figure 3.65) and sella is almost parallel sided (Figure 3.66), which distinguishes it from *R. robinsoni*. Externally this bat also resembles *R. malayanus* in general colouration but differs by its slightly larger size and by the 2nd phalanx of the 3rd finger being over 1.5 times the length of the 1st phalanx whereas it is <1 x this length in *R. malayanus*. Both *R. robinsoni* and *R. malayanus* call at lower echolocation frequencies.

FIGURE 3.64 *Rhinolophus stheno* (Photo Juliana)

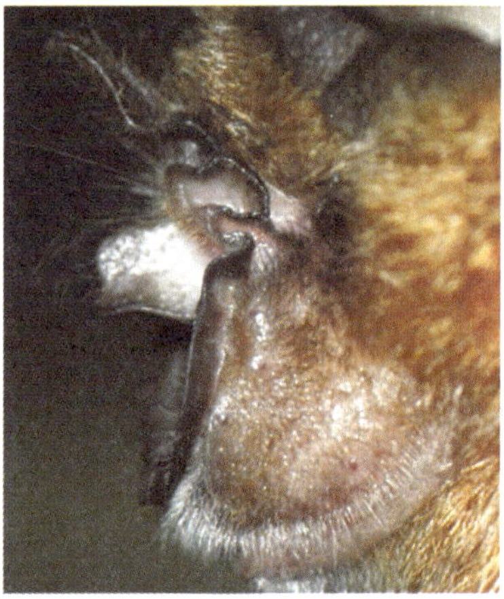

FIGURE 3.65 Side view of *Rhinolophus stheno* to show rounded connecting process (Photo Juliana)

Measurements: (41 specimens) HB 44.0-56.0 mm, T 17.0-20.0 mm, FA 43.5-48.5 mm, Tb 19.0-22.0 mm, E 16.0-20.0 mm, Wt 5.5-11.0 g. KWR: FA 42.9-48.7 mm (n=652), Wt 6.5-12.0 g (n = 642).

Echolocation: CF 86 kHz (Kingston et al. 2000a).

Ecology: An inhabitant of hill and primary forest, found roosting in small numbers in crevices of rock boulders and in larger colonies in caves, where it may roost in association with *Rhinolophus lepidus*. Also netted in the subcanopy of hill forest.

FIGURE 3.66 Sella of *R. stheno* to show roughly parallel sides (Photo Kingston)

Breeding: Of the 27 females examined, 19 females were found pregnant with a single embryo each. February (6 specimens), March (12) and September (1). Medway (1983) recorded that most females examined were pregnant during February-April. At KWR of 51 pregnant females, 31 were captured in March, 19 in April and 1 in May, with lactating females most abundant in May (25), June (36), and July (10).

IUCN: LR (lc).

Distribution KWR (Site, individuals, recaptures): Jenderak Selatan: 58, 12; Kuala Gandah: 179, 23; Kuala Lompat: 186, 38; Kuala Serloh: 149, 24; Lubuk Baung: 287, 31. A very common bat at Kuala Serloh, Kuala Lompat and Lubuk Baung, where it accounts for 12% of individuals (and 9% at Kuala Gandah), this species is much less abundant at Jenderak Selatan, comprising only 3% of individuals. Also captured at Lembah Klau.

Distribution: Vietnam, Thailand, Laos, Peninsular Malaysia, Sumatra, and Java.

Rhinolophus robinsoni Andersen — Peninsular Horseshoe Bat
Kelawar Ladam Semenanjung

Description: A relatively small bat with large, bluntly pointed ears with a prominent antitragus (Figure 3.67). Upperparts dark brown to reddish brown with underparts paler. Noseleaf lacks lateral lappets, connecting process is rounded (Figure 3.68). Sella has a step-wise constriction mid-length that is diagnostic (Figure 3.69). The anterior noseleaf is large covering the muzzle. The lancet is wedge-shaped. Differs from *R. affinis* by its slightly smaller size, and shape of the sella (which has concave sides in *R. affinis*).

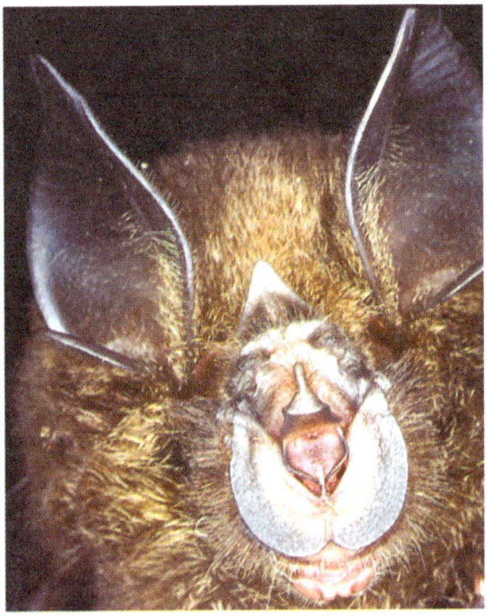

FIGURE 3.67 *Rhinolophus robinsoni* (Photo Kingston)

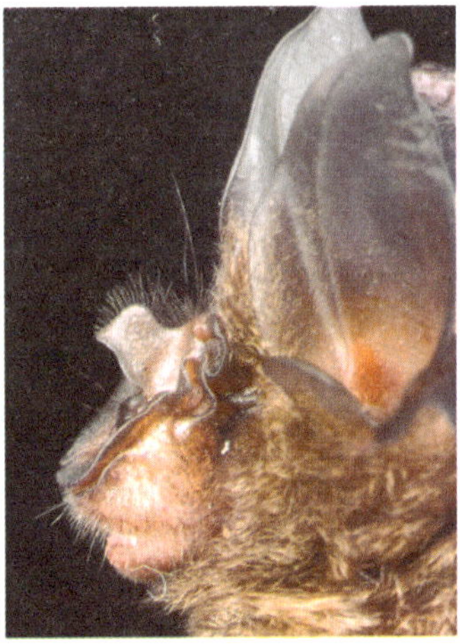

FIGURE 3.68 Side view of *Rhinolophus robinsoni* to show rounded connecting process (Photo Kingston)

Measurements: (6 specimens) HB 47.0-55.0 mm, T 22.0-29.0 mm, FA 40.0-46.0 mm, Tb 17.0-19.0 mm, E 16.0-21.0 mm, Wt 6.0-13.0 g. KWR: FA 42.1-45.4 mm (n = 13), Wt 7.0-10.0 g (n = 14).

FIGURE 3.69 Sella of *Rhinolophus robinsoni* to show step-wise constriction (Photo Kingston)

Echolocation: CF 67 kHz (T. Kingston unpub. data).

Ecology: Primarily a forest species inhabiting lowland and hill forests. Found roosting in crevices of rock boulders, and some individuals have been found hanging from palm leaves in the understorey.

IUCN: LR (lc).

Distribution KWR (Site, individuals, recaptures): Jenderak Selatan: 7, 0; Kuala Serloh: 7, 0; Lubuk Baung: 1, 0. A rare bat, yet to be captured at

Kuala Gandah, but also known from a single individual at Kuala Lompat (Kingston et al. 2003a). DWNP specimens from Bukit Rengit and Kuala Lompat.

Distribution: Peninsular Malaysia, Thailand, and adjacent small islands.

Rhinolophus affinis Horsfield — Intermediate Horseshoe Bat
Kelawar Ladam Hutan

Description: Upperparts dark brown to reddish brown with the hairs darkest at the tips, underparts paler. Noseleaf lacks lateral lappets (Figure 3.70), connecting process is rounded and originates from below the tip of sella (Figure 3.71). The sella is slightly concave (Figure 3.72). The anterior noseleaf is broad, but does not cover the muzzle. Similar in colouration to *R. stheno*, but differs from it by its larger size and concave sella (parallel-sided in *R. stheno*).

Echolocation: CF 78 kHz (Kingston et al. 2000a).

Measurements: (210 specimens) HB 54.0-62.0 mm, T 21.0-27.0 mm, FA 48.0-55.0 mm, Tb 23.0-26.0 mm, E 17.0-22.0 mm, Wt 10.0-15.0 g. KWR: FA 49.8-58.9 mm (n = 22), Wt 12.0-16.0 g (n = 21).

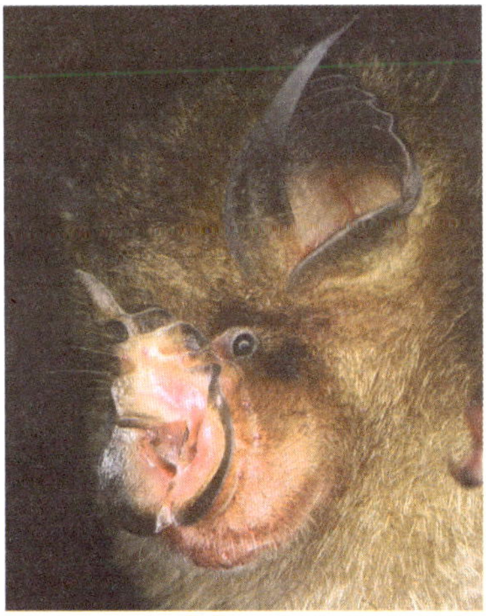

FIGURE 3.70 *Rhinolophus affinis* (Photo Kingston)

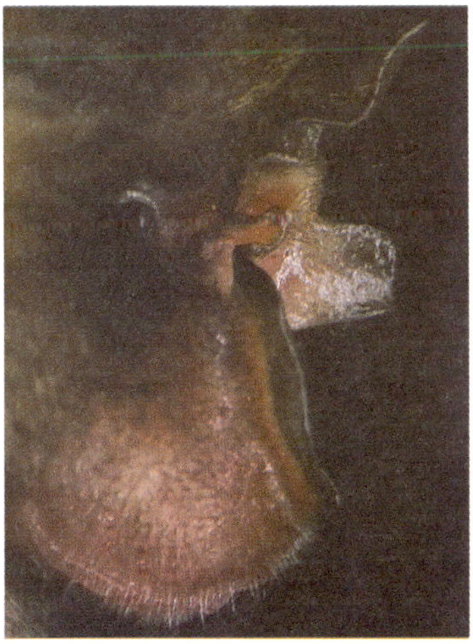

FIGURE 3.71 Side view of *Rhinolophus affinis* to show rounded connecting process (Photo Kingston)

Ecology: Principally a forest species found in primary and secondary forest at all elevations. Gregarious, roosting in large numbers in limestone caves (Medway 1983). Also netted in tall forest at the canopy level.

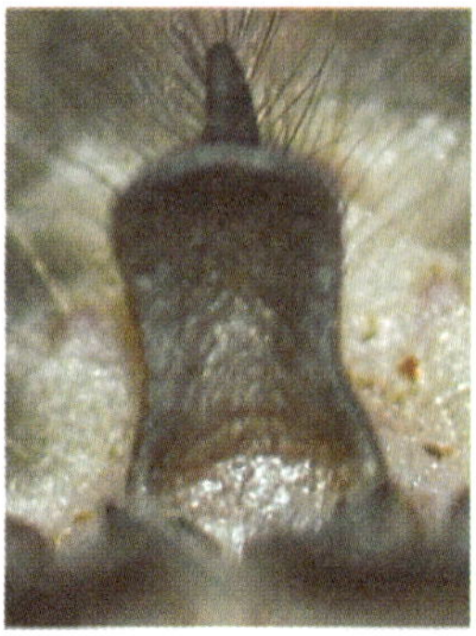

FIGURE 3.72 Concave sella of *Rhinolophus affinis* (Photo Juliana)

Breeding: Of the 134 females examined, 68 were found pregnant with a single embryo each. January (4 specimens), February (3), March (10), April (14), May (3), June (3), July (4), August (3), September (10), October (11), November (5) and December (2). Medway (1983) recorded high pregnancy rates in April-May, October and February-March.

IUCN: LR (lc).

Distribution KWR (Site, individuals, recaptures): Jenderak Selatan: 3, 0; Kuala Gandah: 5, 0; Kuala Lompat: 5, 1; Kuala Serloh: 14, 5. A rare species, not captured at Lubuk Baung and comprising < 0.5% of individuals at Jenderak Selatan, Kuala Gandah and Kuala Lompat. Captures at Kuala Serloh just exceeded 1%. Also captured at Lembah Klau. DWNP specimens from Sg. Chenderoh (Perlok).

Distribution: India and Nepal to S China through Peninsular Malaysia to Borneo and Lesser Sundas Islands, and Andaman Islands (India).

Rhinolophus lepidus Andersen (formerly *R. refulgens*) — Blyth's Horseshoe Bat, Kelawar Ladam Bulu Kilat

Description: A small bat, upperparts are dark grey, brown or reddish brown, occasionally a foxy orange or with a faint silvery sheen, underparts paler (Figure 3.73). Ears and flight membrane dark brown. Noseleaf brown, or pinkish edged with brown, lacking lateral lappets. The connecting process is clearly notched and pointed (Figure 3.74), the sella concave (Figure 3.75).

Echolocation: CF 100 kHz (Kingston et al. 2000a).

FIGURE 3.73 *Rhinolophus lepidus* (Photo Kingston)

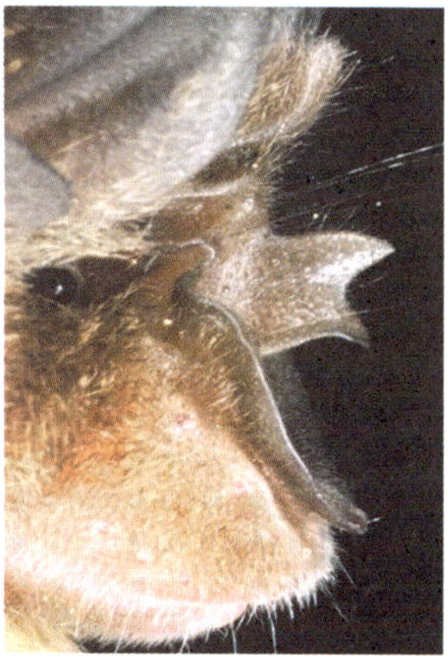

FIGURE 3.74 Side view of notched connecting process of *R. lepidus* (Photo Kingston)

FIGURE 3.75 Sella of *Rhinolophus lepidus* to show concave margins (Photo Kingston)

Measurements: (72 specimens) HB 38.0-50.0 mm, T 15.0-23.0 mm, FA 38.0-42.0 mm, Tb 14.0-19.0 mm, E 14.0-17.0 mm, Wt 4.5-7.5 g. KWR: FA 37.0-43.9 mm (n = 628), Wt 4.5-8.5 g (n = 585).

Ecology: Primarily an inhabitant of lowland forests, but also found in hill forest. Roosts gregariously in crevices of rock boulders and caves, particularly in association with *Rhinolophus stheno*. Medway (1983) recorded individuals in houses as well.

Breeding: Of the 43 females examined, 17 were found pregnant with single foetuses, and two with twin embryos. Pregnancy occurred in the following months: January (3 specimens), March (4), April (1), May (1), August (2), September (2), October (1), November (1), and December (2). Medway (1983) reported most females collected from KWR between February and April 1967 were pregnant, with a single foetus each. KWR: Of 64 lactating females, most were captured in May (25), June (28) and July (10), with pregnancy mainly detected in March (16/37), and April (19/37).

IUCN: LR (lc).

Distribution KWR (Site, individuals, recaptures): Jenderak Selatan: 4, 0; Kuala Gandah: 103, 11; Kuala Lompat: 135, 37; Kuala Serloh: 40, 6; Lubuk Baung: 474, 47. This species shows extreme landscape variability in relative abundance; it was the most common bat at Lubuk Baung, with > 20% of individuals, but comprised only 0.2% of Jenderak Selatan individuals. Abundance at Kuala Serloh was also relatively low (3.4%), but captures at Kuala Gandah and Kuala Lompat comprised 5.4% and 8.7%, respectively, of individuals. Also captured at Lembah Klau. DWNP specimens from Sg. Chenderoh (Perlok) and Kuala Lompat.

Distribution: Afghanistan, N India, Myanmar, Thailand, Szechwan and Yunnan (China), Peninsular Malaysia, and Sumatra.

Rhinolophus acuminatus Peters — Accuminate Horseshoe Bat
Kelawar Ladam Kenarong

Description: Upperparts dark brown to reddish brown, underparts similar or grey to dark brown. Noseleaf, ears and wing membrane dark grey to brown with the membrane arising from the base of toes. Similar in size to *R. macrotis*, differs from it by shorter ears and absence of a cup-like expansion of the nostril margins. The connecting process is clearly notched and pointed (Figure 3.76), the sella parallel-sided (Figure 3.77). Larger than *R. lepidus* which also has a notched connecting process and concave-sided sella.

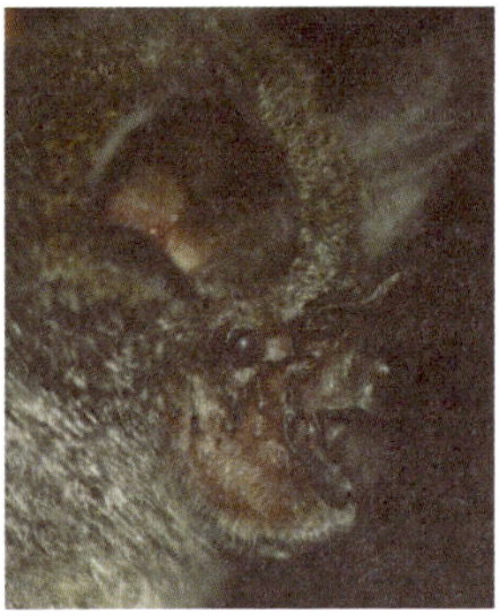

FIGURE 3.76 *Rhinolophus acuminatus* (Photo Juliana)

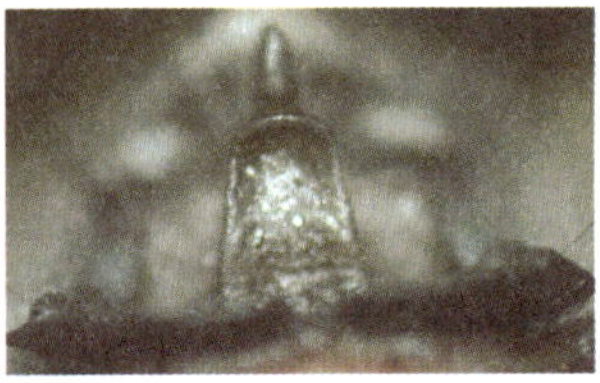

FIGURE 3.77 Parallel-sided sella of *Rhinolophus acuminatus* (Photo Juliana)

Measurements: (30 specimens) HB 50.0-59.0 mm, T 22.0-30.0 mm, FA 45.0-51.0 mm, Tb 18.0-23.0 mm, E 18.0-250 mm, Wt 10.0-16.0 g.

Ecology: The specimens were all collected from primary lowland and hill forests. It has been found roosting either singly or in pairs under palm leaves.

Breeding: Of 13 female specimens examined, two were found pregnant in February and April.

IUCN: LR (lc).

Distribution KWR: A single individual was captured in a house at the Jenderak Selatan Field Station. DWNP specimens from Bukit Rengit and Sg. Chenderoh (Perlok).

Distribution: Thailand, Laos, Cambodia, Peninsular Malaysia Borneo, Sumatra (including Nias and Engano Islands), Java, Lombok, Bali, and the Philippine islands of Palawan, Balabac, and Busuanga.

Family Hipposideridae - Roundleaf Horseshoe Bats

Three genera (*Coelops, Aselliscus and Hipposideros*) and 21 species of Hipposideridae are found in Peninsular Malaysia, of which two genera and 12 species are confirmed for Krau Wildlife Reserve. Like the Rhinolophidae, the noseleaf is complex (Figure 3.18). The anterior noseleaf is rounded and, except in *Coelops* and *Aselliscus*, horseshoe-shaped. There is no sella but a cushion-like median noseleaf that extends laterally for approximately the same width as the anterior noseleaf, as does the posterior noseleaf, a low, rounded projection generally divided by septa into four sections. Crescent-like lateral leaflets are present on the muzzle below the anterior noseleaf in some species. These and the shape of the internarial septa are diagnostic in some species. There is a low antitragus, and the ears vary in size among species. *Coelops* and *Aselliscus* lack a skeletal tail although the interfemoral membranes are well developed.

Coelops robinsoni Bonhote — Malaysian Tailless Horseshoe Bat
Kelawar Dadam Tiada Berekor

Description: A rare, small bat. Hairs on upperparts long and soft, brown to dark brown, dark bases with lighter grey tips. Underparts brownish to ashy. Tailless with the interfemoral membrane well developed. Ears rounded, funnel-shaped with large anti-tragus (Figure 3.78). The noseleaf has wide rounded lappets projecting from the supplementary leaflets flank-

FIGURE 3.78 *Coelops robinsoni* (Photo Kingston)

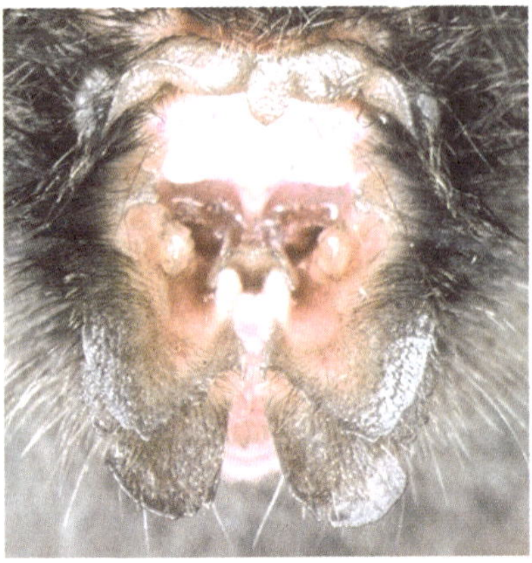

FIGURE 3.79 Noseleaf of *Coelops robinsoni* to show lappets (Photo Kingston)

ing the anterior noseleaf. The anterior noseleaf has a deep median notch extending back to the upper lip with the lateral portions on each side having two superimposed forward-projecting lobes (Figure 3.79). Long thumb supports a large propatagium, and wing tip is short and rounded (Figure 3.80).

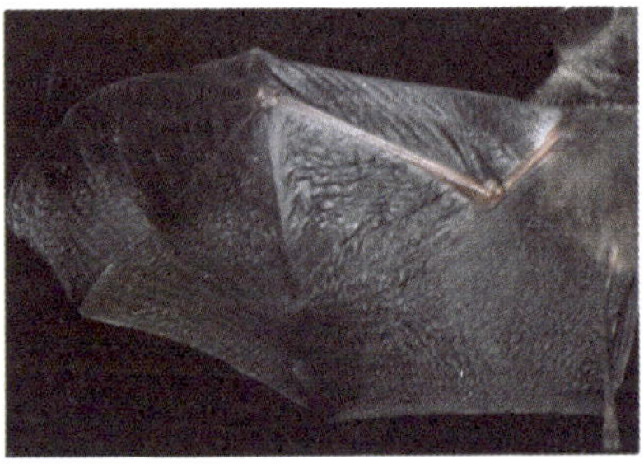

FIGURE 3.80 Left wing of *Coelops robinsoni* showing extensive propatagium, and short, rounded wing tip (Photo Kingston)

Measurements: (3 male specimens KWR) HB 35.0-36.0 mm; T nil; FA 34.0-36.4 mm, Tb 15.0-16.5 mm, E 13.5-15.0 mm, Wt 3.0-4.5 g. KWR 2 pregnant females: FA 34.2-34.9 mm, Wt 4.0 g.

Ecology: All specimens from primary lowland forest. At Lubuk Baung, KWR, a single individual was found roosting in the hollow buttress of a large tree (dbh 130 cm, 30 m height), with a small, ground-level entrance. The roost was also occupied by a male *Hipposideros ridleyi* (C. Fletcher, pers. obs.).

Breeding: Two females at KWR were pregnant in March.

IUCN: LR (nt).

Distribution KWR (Site, individuals, recaptures): Kuala Gandah: 2, 0; Kuala Lompat: 2, 0; Kuala Serloh: 1, 0. A very rare bat with just five individuals captured across three sites.

Distribution: Peninsular Malaysia, Borneo, and Philippines.

Hipposideros lylei Thomas — Shield-faced Roundleaf Bat
Kelawar Muncong Perisai

Description: Upperparts uniformly pale grey to light brown, underparts either paler or buffy brown. Noseleaf is naked and pinkish brown. Ears brown, large and triangular. Flight membrane brown. A sexually dimorphic species, the posterior noseleaf of adult males has an enormous wing-like fleshy expansion projecting well beyond the margin of the posterior noseleaf (Figure 3.81), distinguishing it from all other *Hipposideros*, although this is less pronounced in females (Figure 3.82) and young males. There are two supplementary lateral leaflets on the muzzle on each side of the anterior noseleaf.

Measurements: (2 specimens) HB 75.0-91.0 mm, T 46.0-53.0 mm, FA 77.0-68.0 mm, E 30.0-32.0 mm, Wt 35.0-52.0 g.

Ecology: The two female specimens were collected from caves at Kuala Perlis. Individual netted in lowland primary forest. A single individual was netted in a stacked net system (midstorey to canopy level) at Kuala Lompat.

FIGURE 3.81 Male *Hipposideros lylei* (Photo Wood)

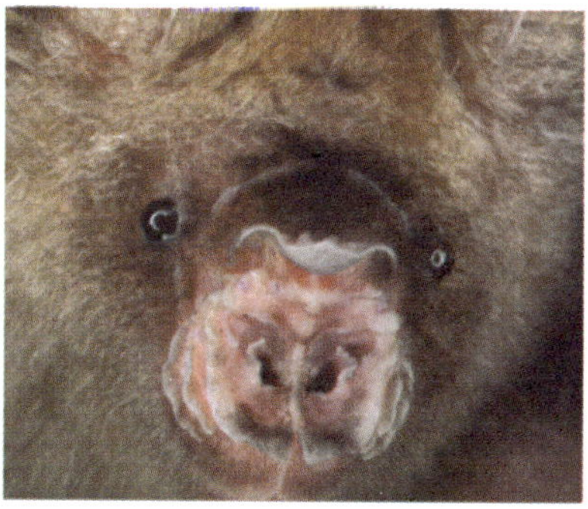

FIGURE 3.82 Female *Hipposideros lylei* (from Myanmar) (Photo Kingston)

Breeding: One of the females was found pregnant in June.

IUCN: LR (nt).

Distribution KWR: A single individual was captured high in the subcanopy in a stacked-net system at Kuala Lompat (R. Hodgkison, per. com.).

Distribution: Myanmar, Thailand, and Peninsular Malaysia.

Hipposideros galeritus Cantor Cantor's Roundleaf Horseshoe Bat
Kelawar Ladam-bulat Pinang

Description: Colour variable with upperparts either grey to reddish or dark brown, underparts paler (Figure 3.83). Ears and wings are brown, noseleaf pinkish-brown. Ears are very broad and short, and distinctly pointed. The anterior noseleaf is well developed and extends almost to the end of the muzzle with two lateral supplementary leaflets. It is similar to *H. cervinus* in body size but has a longer tail, and intermediate noseleaf as wide or wider than the posterior noseleaf.

FIGURE 3.83 *Hipposideros galeritus*. Note two lateral leaflets and intermediate NL wider than posterior NL (Photo Struebig)

Measurements: (8 specimens) HB 45.0-48.0 mm, T 34.0-38.0 mm, FA 45.0-48.0 mm, TB 20.0-21.0 mm, E 15.0-16.0 mm, Wt 6.0-7.5 g. KWR: FA 47.4 mm, Wt 7.7 g (n = 1).

Ecology: All eight specimens were netted in lowland primary forest. They were found not far from large rock boulders. Medway (1983) reported the species as primarily a cave bat and Lekagul and McNeely (1988) found it to roost in small dark chambers deep within cave systems.

Breeding: One of the three females was found pregnant with twin embryos in July.

IUCN: LR (lc).

Distribution KWR: Single records from Kuala Lompat (Kingston et al. 2003a) and Kuala Gandah (2005). Also captured at Lembah Klau. DWNP specimen from Kuala Lompat.

Distribution: Sri Lanka and India through SE Asia to Java and Borneo, and Sanana Islands.

Hipposideros cervinus (Gould) — Fawn-coloured Roundleaf Bat
Kelawar Ladam-bulat Gua

Description: Upperparts vary from brown or grey brown to reddish brown and orange, underparts paler (Figure 3.84). Noseleaf pinkish with two lateral leaflets, intermediate noseleaf narrower than the posterior noseleaf (Figure 3.85), which distinguishes it from *H. galeritus* (as does a shorter tail). The anterior noseleaf is well developed and does not cover the muzzle.

FIGURE 3.84 *Hipposideros cervinus* (Photo Kingston)

Measurements: (85 specimens) HB 47.0-56.0 mm, T 24.0-30.0 mm, FA 48.0-52.0 mm, Tb 15.0-21.0 mm, E 14.0-17.5 mm, Wt 7.0-13.0 g. KWR: FA 44.1-53.0 mm (n – 1,341), Wt 7.0-14.0 g (n = 1,234).

Echolocation: CF 126 kHz (Kingston et al. 2000a).

Ecology: A common bat usually found roosting gregariously in large colonies than can exceed 100,000 in limestone caves, or caves and crevices amongst boulders, sometimes in association with *H. bicolor*. In primary lowland and hill forests, commonly netted and trapped in the forest understorey.

Breeding: Of the 38 females examined, 10 were found to be pregnant with a single embryo each, March (4 specimens), April (5), and August (1). KWR: Lactating females were found throughout the year but with a peak May-July (247/280), with corresponding peaks in pregnancy in February-March (97/105).

FIGURE 3.85 Face of *H. cervinus*. Note two lateral leaflets and width of intermediate NL < posterior (Photo Kingston)

IUCN: LR (lc).

Distribution KWR (Site, individuals, recaptures): Jenderak Selatan: 1,252, 489; Kuala Gandah: 535, 64; Kuala Lompat: 142, 44; Kuala Serloh: 135, 12; Lubuk Baung: 207, 38. The dominant species at Jenderak Selatan where the presence of a boulder cave formation just off the grid likely explains the high catch rate (66% of individuals). It is also the most common bat at Kuala Gandah (28%) and remains common at Kuala Lompat (9%), Kuala Serloh (11%) and Lubuk Baung (8%). Also captured at Lembah Klau. DWNP specimens from Bukit Rengit and Sg. Chenderoh (Perlok).

Distribution: Peninsular Malaysia, Sumatra, Philippines through to Vanuatu, and NE Australia.

Hipposideros larvatus (Horsfield) Large Roundleaf Horseshoe Bat
Kelawar Ladam-bulat Besar

Description: Upperparts are light brown, golden brown to dark or reddish brown and occasionally bright orange (through cave bleaching effects) (Figure 3.86). In some individuals the fur tips are paler giving a slightly frosted appearance. Underparts paler (from pale brown, pale orange to greyish brown). The wings are brown. The noseleaf and three lateral leaflets are pinkish brown or pink edged with brown (Figure 3.87); the anterior noseleaf is fairly large, but does not expand to cover the muzzle. The ears are brown and distally triangular with a low, but sharply pointed antitragus, rather like *H. cervinus*.

FIGURE 3.86 *Hipposideros larvatus* (Photo: Juliana)

FIGURE 3.87 Face of *Hipposideros larvatus* (Photo Juliana)

Measurements: (83 specimens) HB 53.0-68.0 mm, T 30.0-41.0 mm, FA 56.0-62.0 mm, Tb 22.0-26.0 mm, E 17.0-21.0 mm, Wt 16.0-19.0 g. KWR: FA 57.1-61.8 mm, Wt 14.3-20.5 g (n = 26).

Echolocation: CF 100 kHz (Kingston et al. 2000a).

Ecology: A common inhabitant of limestone caves. Also found in crevices of large rock boulders in both primary and secondary forest at all elevations. In caves they roost in large colonies.

Breeding: Of 33 adult females examined, 19 were found to be pregnant with a single embryo each. February (4 specimens), April (6), July (4), August (2), and December (3). Four specimens were found with attached pups. KWR: 8 lactating females - July (2), August (5), and October (1).

Distribution KWR: Currently only reported for Kuala Lompat (3 individuals) and Lubuk Baung (25). An additional 22 captures for Kuala Lompat are given by Kingston et al. (2003a).

Distribution: N and E India, Bangladesh, Yunnan, Kwangsi and Hainan (China), Laos, Peninsular Malaysia to Sumatra, Java, Borneo, and adjacent small islands including Kangean Islands(Indonesia).

Hipposideros diadema (Geoffroy) Diadem Roundleaf Bat
Kelawar Ladam-bulat Terbesar

Description: A large bat, with fur on upperparts tricoloured: brown at the base, then white-buff followed by brown-chestnut (Figure 3.88). White flash on side of shoulders which continues along dorsal side of body (where wing membrane joins body) (Figure 3.89). In females there is an orange tinge to fur, especially apparent in those parts that are buffy or cream in males. The head is buffy-brown (brown bases) with brown stripe running centrally from top of head to nose, but this may be pale in some individuals. Noseleaf is pinkish with ears and wings brown, fingers slightly lighter brown. The posterior noseleaf is rounded and larger than the anterior leaf which has 3-4 (usually 4) supplementary leaflets on each side; the outer one may be rudimentary (Figure 3.89). Median noseleaf with median ridge. The large size and white shoulder patches distinguish it from all other species, although *H. armiger* is slightly larger, it is uniformly dark brown.

FIGURE 3.88 *Hipposideros diadema* (Photo Juliana)

Measurements: (30 specimens) HB 80.0-96.0 mm, T 49.0-55.0 mm, FA 80.0-88.5 mm, Tb 35.0-38.0 mm, E 25.0-31.0 mm, Wt 35.0-55.0 g. KWR: FA 78.0-90.6 mm (n = 102), Wt 34.0-58.0 g (n = 95).

Echolocation: CF 60 kHz (Kingston et al. 2000a).

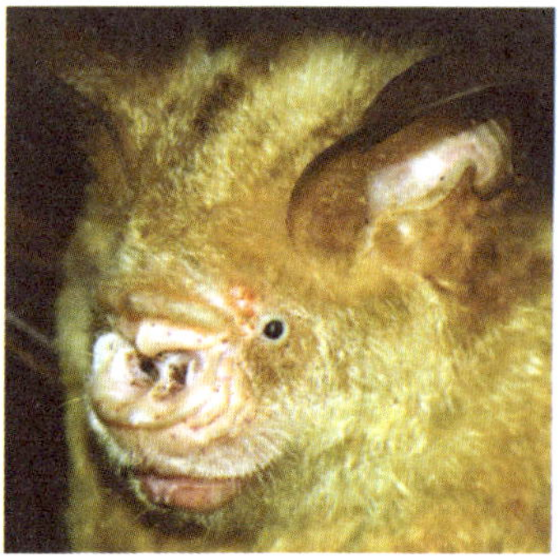

FIGURE 3.89 Face of *Hipposideros diadema* (Photo Juliana)

Ecology: Primarily a cave dweller and highly gregarious and abundant in caves of limestone hills. Also found roosting in small colonies in crevices of large boulders, and occasionally found solitary under palms, or roosting at the final feeding perch in the forest midstorey. It is common in both primary and secondary forest at all elevations. Forages primarily by perch hunting in gaps in the midstorey or over trails, waiting for slow-flying insects to pass beneath. In Australia the diet is primarily beetles, moths, and orthopterans, with evidence of occasional carnivory on birds (Pavey & Burwell 1997). In Malaysia, diet also includes termites during swarming periods. Radio-tracking of a single male at Kuala Lompat found that the bat rotated through several perches in a night, all within approximately a 1 km^2 area. During the day, the bat roosted alone, below leaves of the midstorey at or near the last feeding perch (T. Kingston, unpub. data).

Breeding: Five of the 10 females examined were pregnant with a single embryo each. March (1 specimen), April (2), May (1) and July (1). Medway (1983) reported females and young bats present in March and April from Batu Caves, Selangor. KWR: lactating females from February-July (10), pregnant March, and April (8).

IUCN: LR (lc).

Distribution KWR (Site, individuals, recaptures): Jenderak Selatan: 16, 1; Kuala Gandah: 12, 7; Kuala Lompat: 45, 11; Kuala Serloh: 20, 3; Lubuk Baung: 23, 1. Present in moderately low numbers on all grids, accounting for 0.6% (Kuala Gandah) to 2.9% (Kuala Lompat) of individuals. Recapture rates are high for Kuala Gandah and Kuala Lompat. DWNP specimens from Bukit Rengit, Sg. Chenderoh (Perlok), Lembah Klau.

Distribution: Myanmar and Vietnam through Thailand, Laos, Peninsular Malaysia and Indonesia to New Guinea, Bismarck Arch., Solomon Islands and NE Australia, Philippines, and Nicobar Islands.

Hipposideros armiger (Hodgson) Great Roundleaf Horseshoe Bat
Kelawar Ladam-bulat Besar

Description: This is the largest of the Hipposideridae in Peninsular Malaysia. Upperparts are uniformly dark brown to dark reddish brown, underparts either dark brown or slightly paler. Ears, noseleaf and wings are

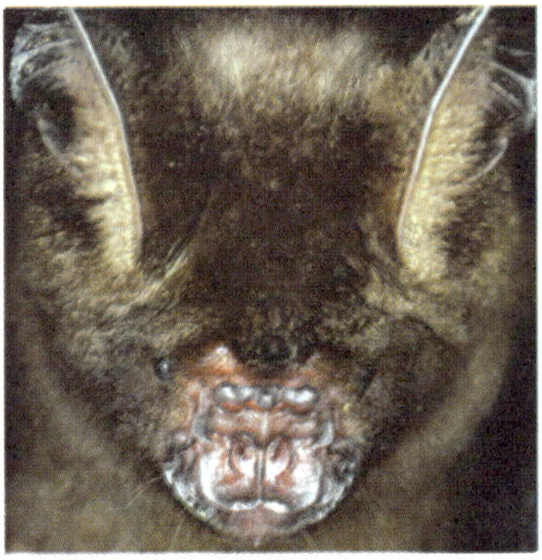

FIGURE 3.90 *Hipposideros armiger* (Photo Kingston)

FIGURE 3.91 Colony of *Hipposideros armiger* in a cave (Photo Juliana)

dark brown. Transverse fleshy structures arise behind the posterior noseleaf on each side, and the upper margins of the posterior leaf are thickened and form three rounded lobes (Figure 3.90). The anterior noseleaf is much wider than the posterior with four lateral supplementary leaflets on each side (although the outermost is often rudimentary). The tip of the tail is free from the interfemoral membrane. Differs from the *H. diadema* by colour and slightly larger size.

Echolocation: 74 kHz in China (Zhang et al. 2000).

Measurements: (16 specimens) HB 85.0-100.0 mm, T 47.0-65.0 mm, FA 85.0-97.0 mm, Tb 38.0-45.0 mm, E 26.0-35.0 mm, Wt 40.0-64.0 g.

Ecology: Primarily a cave dweller (Figure 3.91), also found in crevices of large boulders in primary and secondary forest at all elevations. In caves, they roost in large numbers preferably in large chambers, and often share roosts with other species. Solitary individuals were also found hanging onto a bertam tree in forest. A study by Zubaid (1988) at Bukit Siam, Perlis, found that a large proportion of diet was Coleoptera (36.7%) and Hymenoptera (28.8%) - predominantly carpenter bees (Xylocopini) - with lesser amounts of Orthoptera, Isoptera, Homoptera, Odonata, Diptera and Lepidoptera. The presence of diurnal species and those most commonly found on surfaces suggests the ability to glean (Zubaid 1988).

Breeding: Three of the five females examined were pregnant with a single embryo each. April (1 specimen), May (1), September (2), and November (2). Based on records from 1950-1964 Medway (1983) found pregnant females from February-May and September-October indicating two annual breeding seasons.

IUCN: LR (lc).

Distribution KWR: An adult male was captured at a cave near Kuala Serloh. Several captured at Lembah Klau. Medway and Wells (1971) also report this species for KWR.

Distribution: N India, Nepal, Myanmar, S and SE China, Vietnam, Laos, Cambodia, Thailand, Peninsular Malaysia, and Taiwan.

Hipposideros ridleyi Robinson and Kloss — Ridley's Roundleaf Horseshoe Bat, Kelawar Ladam-bulat Singapore

FIGURE 3.92 *Hipposideros ridleyi* (Photo Kingston)

Description: Upperparts uniformly dark brown, underparts slightly paler. Ears, noseleaf and wing membrane dark grey to brown. Ears large and rounded (Figure 3.92). The noseleaf is very large, and the internarial septum is expanded to form a concave disk that is diagnostic. No lateral leaflets.

Measurements: (14 specimens) HB 48.0-56.0 mm, T 27.0-30.0 mm, FA 47.0-51.0 mm, Tb 21.0-23.0 mm, E 24.0-28.0 mm, Wt 8.0-12.5 g. KWR: FA 46.5-51.9 mm (n = 104), Wt 7.5-13.5 g (n = 101).

Echolocation: CF 62 kHz (Kingston et al. 2000a).

Ecology: A primary forest species, also found roosting in small groups of up to 15 individuals (females) in culverts and drainage tunnels (Gould

1978c). In KWR, 10 females and four males were radio-tracked to 14 roosts, 13 of which were deep hollows (> 8 m length) in large (up to 30 m; DBH typically > 100 cm) fallen trees (Figure 3.93). Females were most commonly found in all-female/juvenile groups of four to seven individuals (Figure 3.94), and were only occasionally found roosting with adult males. Three of the four males were found roosting alone, one in the hollow of a large living tree that was also occupied by at least one *Coelops robinsoni.*

FIGURE 3.93 *Hipposideros ridleyi* roost at Lubuk Baung (Photo Fletcher)

Breeding: One of the females was pregnant with a single embryo in March. KWR: lactating February (1), May (6), Jun (6), July (4), August (3), September (6), and October (2); pregnant March (2), April (2), and May (1).

IUCN: Vulnerable (B1 + 2c)

Distribution KWR (Site, individuals, recaptures): Jenderak Selatan: 3, 0; Kuala Gandah: 25, 9; Kuala Lompat: 30, 9; Kuala Serloh: 30, 16; Lubuk Baung: 37, 10. Rarely captured at Jenderak Selatan, elsewhere this species comprised from 1.3% (Kuala Gandah) to 2.5% (Kuala Serloh) of individuals. Recapture rates high, particularly at Kuala Serloh. DWNP specimens from Kuala Lompat.

FIGURE 3.94 *Hipposideros ridleyi* colony inside roost (Photo Fletcher)

Distribution: Peninsular Malaysia, Borneo.

Hipposideros doriae (Peters) — Least Roundleaf Bat
(formerly *H. sabanus*) — Kelawar Ladam-bulat Lawas

Description: A very small bat. Upperparts are dark brown to buffy brown, underparts paler. Ears comparatively large and rounded. Noseleaf very small and simple with no lateral leaflets. Similar to *H. bicolor* and *H. cineraceus* in external characteristics, but smaller and lacks the vertical septa on the posterior noseleaf.

Measurements: (8 specimens) HB 34.0-45.0 mm, T 34.0-37.0 mm, FA 34.0-37.1 mm, Tb 14.0-17.0 mm, E 14.0-17.0 mm, Wt 4.0-5.0 g. KWR: FA 33.6-39.1 mm (n = 19), Wt 4.0-6.0 g (n = 14).

Echolocation: 195-200 kHz (Kingston et al. 2000a).

Ecology: The specimens were collected in lowland to submontane forests up to 1500 m in elevation.

Breeding: One of the two females was pregnant with a single embryo in February. KWR: three pregnant females captured in May, one in April.

Distribution KWR (Site, individuals, recaptures): Jenderak Selatan: 6, 2; Kuala Gandah: 8, 1; Kuala Lompat: 5, 2; Kuala Serloh: 2, 0; Lubuk Baung: 3, 0. Present, but rare at all sites (< 0.5% of individuals). DWNP specimens from Kuala Lompat and Bukit Tapah (near Bukit Rengit).

Distribution: Borneo, Sumatra, and Peninsular Malaysia.

Hipposideros cineraceus Blyth — Least Roundleaf Horseshoe Bat
Kelawar Ladam-bulat Kecil

Description: A small bat. Upperparts buffy-brown to dark brown (Figure 3.95), underparts buffy brown to pale brown; fur bicoloured with white bases (Figure 3.96). Wings brown, ears are large and rounded to a point and are brown/grey with pale bases. The noseleaf is simple, pinkish or pink edged with grey/black, and closely resembles that of *H. bicolor*, but the internarial septum is thickened in the middle to form a slightly raised bump (Figure 3.97). It is also distinguished from *H. bicolor* by the smaller body size, and from *H. sabanus* by the presence of vertical septa.

FIGURE 3.95 *Hipposideros cineraceus* (Photo Kingston)

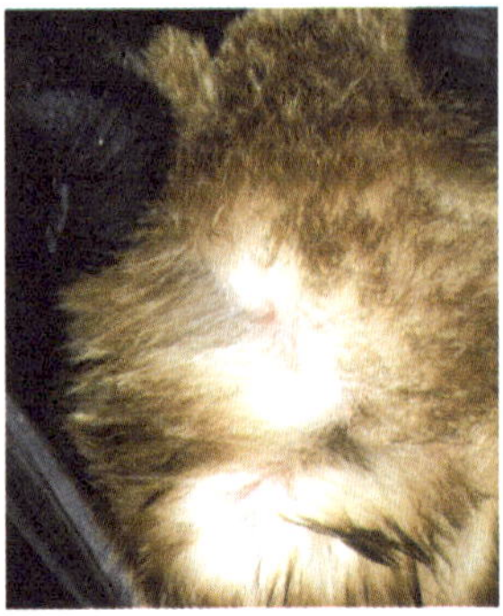

FIGURE 3.96 Bicoloured dorsal fur of *Hipposideros cineraceus* (Photo Kingston)

Measurements: (12 specimens) HB 36.0-45.0 mm, T 24.0-28.0 mm, FA 35.0-38.0 mm, Tb 15.0-17.0 mm, E 14.0-17.0 mm, Wt 4.0-5.0 g.

Echolocation: CF 144 kHz (Kingston et al. 2000a).

Ecology: Primarily a cave dweller, roosting gregariously in association with other *Hipposideros*. It is found in forest at all elevations. At Kuala Lompat two females with young were found roosting in a culvert in the grounds of the field station.

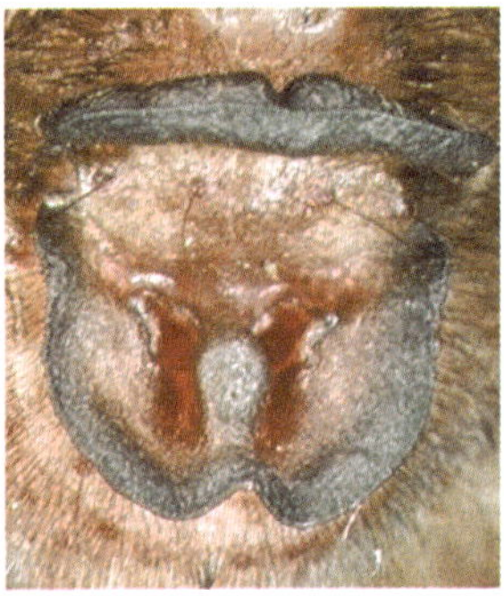

FIGURE 3.97 Noseleaf of *H. cineraceus*. Note slight raised bump of internarial septum (Photo Kingston)

Breeding: Four of the nine females were found to be pregnant with a single embryo each. April (2 specimens), June (1) and September (1). Medway (1983) reported young born in April.

IUCN: LR (lc).

Distribution KWR (Site, individuals, recaptures): Jenderak Selatan: 1, 0; Kuala Gandah: 3, 0; Kuala Serloh: 2, 0; Lubuk Baung: 2, 0. Also recorded at Kuala Lompat by Kingston et al. (2003a), but rare at all sites. DWNP specimens from Kuala Lompat.

Distribution: Pakistan and India to Myanmar, Thailand, Laos, Vietnam, Sumatra and Borneo and adjacent small islands including Kangean Islands (Indonesia).

*Hipposideros bicolor*Temminck Bicoloured Roundleaf Horseshoe Bat
Kelawar Ladam-bulat Biasa

Comprises a pair of cryptic species that are genetically and acoustically divergent, but show morphological overlap. Until the taxonomy is reviewed fully they are denoted as phonic types based on the mean frequency of the CF component of the calls: *H. bicolor* 142-kHz and H. bicolor 131-kHz (Kingston et al. 2001). Bats with a FA < 43 mm and Tb < 19 mm can be assigned to *H. bicolor* 142 kHz with a high degree of confidence, and those with FA > 45 mm and Tb > 20 mm to *H. bicolor* 131 kHz, but intermediates are difficult to distinguish without knowledge of call frequency.

Description: Upperparts buffy brown to greyish brown or chestnut to orange (presumably due to bleaching in roosts) (Figure 3.98). Underparts paler or buffy white. Fur is distinctly bicoloured, with white bases. Ears large and rounded. Noseleaf, ears and flight membrane are brown. The noseleaf is small and simple, lacking lateral leaflets with a straight internarial septum. The noseleaf of the 142-kHz bat is slightly curved up at the margins, while that of the 131-kHz bat is slightly flatter, but this is difficult to distinguish without both phonic types in the hand (Figure 3.99).

Measurements: 131-kHz bats from KWR: FA 43.0-48.9 mm, Tb 18.8-22.6 mm, Wt 7.0-10.0 g (n = 33). 142-kHz bats from KWR: FA 41.1-45.0 mm (n = 52), Tb 17.7-20.0 mm (n = 48), Wt 7.0 - 10.5 g (n = 49).

Echolocation: 131 kHz bat: 127.0 - 134. 4 kHz (n = 27); 142 kHz bats 138.0 - 144.0 kHz (n = 53) (Kingston et al. 2001, and T. Kingston unpub. data).

Ecology: Primarily cave dwellers, roosting in large colonies together. Also found in crevices of large boulders in primary and hill forests.

IUCN (as *H. bicolor*): LR (lc).

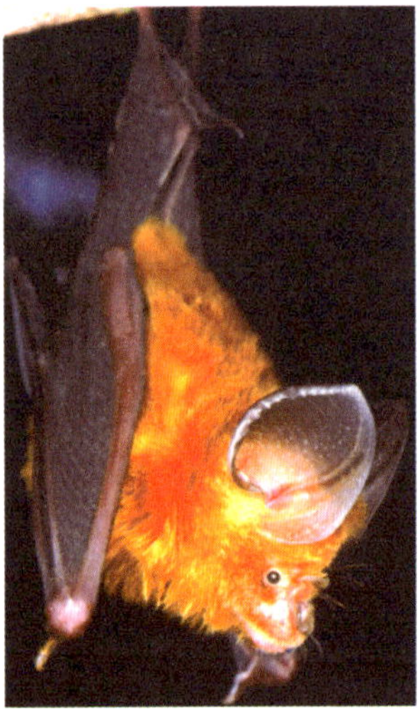

FIGURE 3.98 *Hipposideros bicolor* 142-kHz (Photo Kingston)

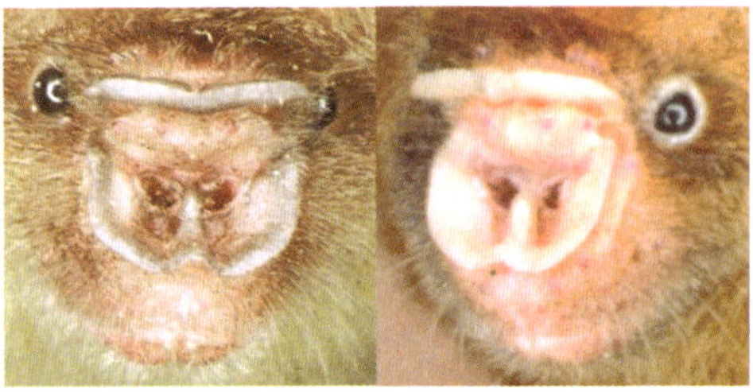

FIGURE 3.99 Noseleaves of *Hipposideros bicolor* 142-kHz (left) and *Hipposideros bicolor* 131-kHz (right) (Photos Kingston)

Distribution KWR (Site, individuals, recaptures): 131-kHz bat: Jenderak Selatan: 262, 14; Kuala Gandah: 85, 28; Kuala Lompat: 36, 3; Kuala Serloh: 20, 2; Lubuk Baung: 27, 5. 142-kHz bat: Jenderak Selatan: 117, 20; Kuala Gandah: 16, 3; Kuala Lompat: 24, 5; Kuala Serloh: 5, 0; Lubuk Baung: 171, 33. Both species were found in high numbers at Jenderak Selatan, although the 131-kHz bat was the more abundant (131-kHz - 14%, 142-kHz - 6%), as it was at Kuala Gandah (4% vs. 1%), Kuala Serloh and Kuala Lompat. However, the 142-kHz bat was by far the more common at Lubuk Baung (7% vs. 1%). Both captured at Lembah Klau.

Distribution (as *H. bicolor*): Laos, Vietnam, S Thailand, Peninsular Malaysia to Borneo and the Philippines, Java, Sumbawa, Seralu, Sumba, Savu, Roti, and Timor Islands (Indonesia), and adjacent small islands.

Family Vespertilionidae - Evening Bats

Nearly half the insectivorous bats in Peninsular Malaysia belong to this family. There are at least 42 species in Peninsular Malaysia belonging to 14 genera in four subfamilies. The diagnostic feature for the family in Malaysia is a long tail that is completely enclosed in the interfemoral membrane and a simple nose, without noseleaf.

Subfamily Miniopterinae - Long-fingered or Bent-winged Bats

Represented by a single genus, *Miniopterus*, there are three species in Peninsular Malaysia, two of which are confirmed for KWR. All *Miniopterus* species are characterised by the third finger with a short first phalanx and a very long terminal phalanx that is three times the length of the first, causing the wing to bend up at the third finger when at rest. Skull measurements may be necessary to confirm identifications as there is often overlap of forearm and weight among species.

Miniopterus schreibersii (Kuhl) — Schreiber's Long-fingered Bat
Kelawar Jari Panjang Bukit

FIGURE 3.100 *Miniopterus schreibersii* (Photo Kingston)

Description: Upperparts dark reddish brown, underparts paler in colour. Flight membrane blackish. The fur is dense, but the muzzle is generally without fur (Figure 3.100). The tragus is club-shaped and bent forwards.

Measurements: (11 specimens) HB 48.0-56.0 mm, T 37.0-45.0 mm, FA 42.5-45.0 mm, Tb 16.0-18.0 mm, E 9.0-10.0 mm, Wt 11.0-13.0 g.

Ecology: Based on the present specimens, nine out of the eleven individuals were netted from hill and montane type terrain. Medway (1983) reported that these bats were gregarious, roosting in caves in large colonies. At KWR, this species has been netted over rivers.

IUCN: LR (nt).

Distribution KWR: Captured in mist nets set over rivers at Kuala Gandah, Kuala Lompat and Lubuk Baung (T. Wood unpub. data).

Distribution: S Europe and Morocco through the Caucasus, Iran, Bulgaria to most of China and Japan; most of Indo-Malayan region, Philippines, New Guinea, Solomon Islands (including Bougainville Island), Australia, sub-Saharan Africa, and Bismarck Arch.

Miniopterus medius Thomas and Wroughton — Intermediate Long-fingered Bat, Kelawar Jari Panjang

Description: Upperparts dark brown to reddish brown or black. The wings and interfemoral membrane are blackish. Distinguished from *M. schreibersii* by smaller size (but care needed as there may be some overlap).

Measurements: (6 specimens) HB 40.0-52.0 mm, T 38.0-50.0 mm, FA 36.0-41.0 mm, Tb 14.0-16.0 mm, E 10.0-12.0 mm, Wt. 5.9-11.0 g. KWR: FA 43.1 mm, Wt 8.7 g (n = 1).

Echolocation: Frequency-modulated sweeps of average duration 3 ms, starting at 67 kHz and ending in a constant frequency component with a peak frequency of 57 kHz and end frequency 55 kHz (13 individuals, 195 calls, recorded flying 5-10 m above ground) (T. Wood unpub. data).

Ecology: This bat is primarily a forest species and is found from lowland to hill and montane forests. Medway (1983) recorded bats roosting in caves in great numbers. Based on the present collection it is observed that this species is not common.

IUCN: LR (lc).

Distribution KWR: A single individual was captured in a harp trap at Kuala Lompat (Kingston et al. 2003a).

Distribution: SE China, Thailand, Peninsular Malaysia, Borneo, Java, Sulawesi, Philippines, and New Guinea.

Subfamily Murininae - Tube-nosed Bats

Represented by two genera, *Murina* and *Harpiocephalus* with all six species from Peninsular Malaysia found in KWR. All species possess prominent tubular nostrils and rounded ears with long pointed tragus with a notch at the base of the posterior margin.

Harpiocephalus mordax — Thomas Hairy-winged Bat
Kelawar Sayap Berbulu

Description: A colourful bat with the fur on the upperparts bright orange with the underparts similar in colour but slightly paler. Wing membrane is dark brownish. The forearm and much of the interfemoral membrane are covered with short orange hairs. Distinguished from *Murina* spp. by large size.

Measurements: (5 specimens) HB 65.0-75.0 mm, T 54.0-58.0 mm, FA 48.5-52.5 mm, Tb 24.0-26.0 mm, E 15.0-18.5 mm, Wt 19.0-25.5 g.

Ecology: The species has so far been netted in tall forests or hilly elevations. It is uncommon and hardly anything is known of its ecology.

Breeding: One of three females examined was pregnant in August.

IUCN: LR (nt).

Distribution KWR: A very rare bat with just two individuals recorded, one at Kuala Serloh, the other at Jenderak Selatan.

Distribution: Myanmar, Thailand, Peninsular Malaysia, Vietnam, and Borneo.

Murina cyclotis — Dobson's Round-eared Tube-nosed Bat
Kelawar Hidong-laras Telinga

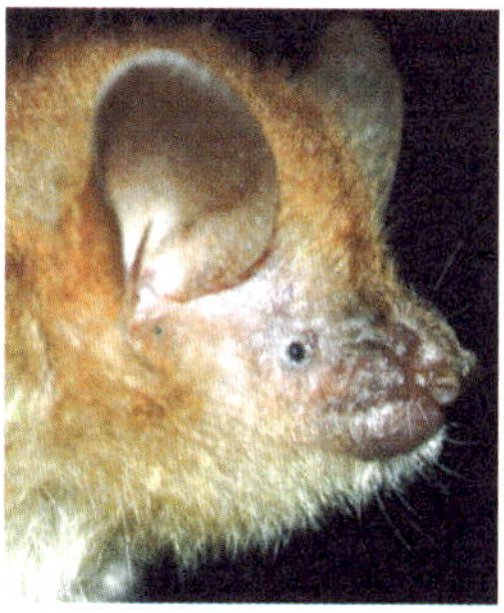

FIGURE 3.101 *Murina cyclotis* (Photo Juliana)

Description: Fur on upperparts very soft and long, orange-brown with paler grey bases (Figure 3.101). Fur extends onto arm wing and uropatagium which is lightly haired to the end; toes haired, forearm lightly haired. Underparts paler in colour; buffy-yellow with pale bases to hairs. Wing and interfemoral membrane dark to light brown, except around fingers where skin is slightly translucent. Ears rounded, light brown and whitish at base internally, while the long pointed tragus (slightly curved, and not as narrow as *Kerivoula*) is white with brown tips, with a notch at the base of the posterior margin (like that of *Phoniscus*). Distinguished from all other *Murina* by large size.

Measurements: (16 specimens) HB 43.0-58.0 mm, T 39.0-51.0 mm, FA 35.0-44.5 mm, Tb 18.0-22.0 mm, E 11.0-15.0 mm, Wt 6.7-12.3 g. KWR: FA 32.1-40.9 mm (n = 126), Wt 6.5-13 g (n = 127).

Echolocation: High frequency, very broadband FM sweeps, of low intensity and short duration, and typically emitted in groups of 1-2 calls. Mean initial frequency 165 kHz, terminal frequency 52 kHz, peak frequency 77 kHz (but energy distributed fairly evenly throughout call), duration around 2 ms (1-4 ms) (Kingston et al. 1999).

Ecology: This bat is found mainly in primary forests ranging from lowland, hill and montane terrain. Medway (1983) reported specimens collected in forests from the foothills up to 1,370 m. Captured relatively frequently in harp traps in the understorey of primary forest at KWR. There is little information of its roosting habits, but one individual was observed flying from a wild banana tree and was accidentally caught by a net placed nearby.

Breeding: One of the three females examined was pregnant in December. Medway (1983) recorded pregnant females in February and May carrying two foetuses with one in each uterine horn. Lactating females were captured in KWR in March (1), April (2), May (5), June (1), and July (1).

IUCN: LR (lc).

Distribution KWR (Site, individuals, recaptures): Jenderak Selatan: 34, 6; Kuala Gandah: 19, 4; Kuala Lompat: 30, 12; Kuala Serloh: 14, 0; Lubuk Baung: 46, 6. Generally less common that the smaller *Murina suilla* (except at Lubuk Baung), with abundance of individuals between 1-2%. Also captured at Lembah Klau. DWNP specimens from Bukit Rengit and Sg. Chenderoh (Perlok).

Distribution: Sri Lanka and India to Kwangtung and Hainan (China); Myanmar, Laos, and Vietnam, south to Peninsular Malaysia, Borneo, Sumatra, Philippines, and Lesser Sunda Islands.

Murina aenea Hill

Bronzed Tube-nosed Bat
Kelawar Bulu Emas

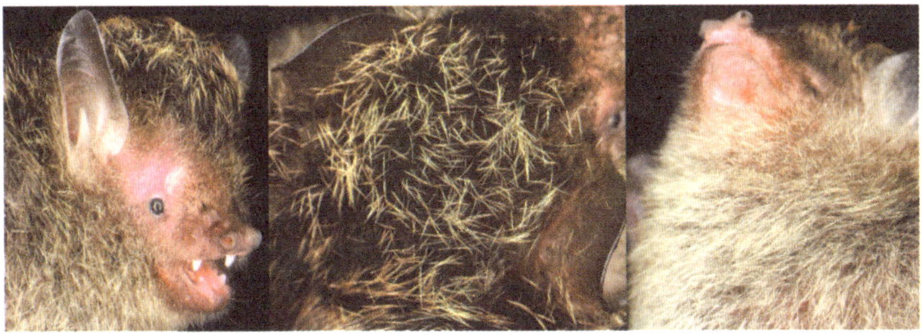

Figure 3.102 *Murina aenea* (left), showing bronze tips on upperparts (centre) and buffy underparts (right) (Photos Kingston)

Description: Fur on upperparts tricoloured - brown/black bases with buffy-brown middle and brown/black tips (variable), then bronze tipping giving an overall gold appearance (Figure 3.102). Underparts paler, buffy banded with buffy brown, or yellow-orange tips (bases always darker). Tibia and tail membrane are lightly furred with bronze hairs, as are the forearm and wrist. Ears brown with paler bases; tragus pale, without coloured tips and with a notch in the posterior margin at the base. Small gland at the base of penis. Similar in size to *M. cyclotis* but distinguished by fur colour, and from *M. huttoni* by colour and shorter forearm length. Differs from *M. rozendaali* in size (larger FA), and more buff underparts (which are yellowish in *M. rozendaali*) which grade smoothly into upperparts.

Measurements: (6 specimens) HB 42.0-50.0 mm, T 37.0-43.0 mm, FA 34.0-37.0 mm, Tb 16.0-20.5 mm, E 12.0-15.5 mm, Wt 6.6-10.3 g. KWR: FA 33.9-37.1 mm, Wt 5.8-8.5 g (n = 19).

Echolocation: High frequency, very broadband FM sweeps, of low intensity and short duration, and typically emitted in groups 1-2 calls. Mean initial frequency 152 kHz, terminal frequency 43 kHz, peak frequency 83 kHz (but energy distributed fairly evenly throughout call), duration 2-3 ms (Kingston et al. 1999).

Ecology: The present specimens were all collected from primary lowland forests. Medway (1983) recorded specimens collected at lowland and hill forests as well. Captured rarely at KWR.

Breeding: One of the two females examined was pregnant in the month of June. KWR: lactating female in March.

IUCN: LR (nt).

Distribution KWR (Site, individuals, recaptures): Jenderak Selatan: 5, 0; Kuala Gandah: 6, 1; Kuala Lompat: 3, 1; Kuala Serloh: 5, 0; Lubuk Baung: 2, 1. Present but rare at all sites (< 0.5% of individuals).

Distribution: Peninsular Malaysia, and Borneo.

Murina suilla — Temminck Brown Tube-nosed Bat
Kelawar Hidung Lawas Kecil

FIGURE 3.103 *Murina suilla* (Photo Kingston)

Description: Fur on upperparts tricoloured - base grey, middle buffy/orange, tips brown orange or brown grey (Figure 3.103). Overall appears brown with an orange hue in some individuals, underparts greyish white (Figure 3.104). Fur extends onto arm wing and uropatagium; tibia furred. Wings dark brown/black. Arm wing joins at base of toes. Ears brown, tragus pale or white with brown tip. Distinguished by being the smallest in size amongst the *Murina* species.

FIGURE 3.104 *Murina suilla* - browner form (Photo Kingston)

Measurements: (12 specimens) HB 34.0-40.0 mm, T 26.0-38.0 mm, FA 28.0-30.0 mm, Tb 14.0-15.0 mm, E 10.0-13.0 mm, Wt 3.0-

4.7 g. KWR: FA 25.8-32.5 mm (n = 212), Wt 2.5-5.5 g (n = 201).

Echolocation: High frequency, very broadband FM sweeps, of low intensity and short duration, and typically emitted in groups 1-2 calls. Mean initial frequency 165 kHz, terminal frequency 55 kHz, peak frequency 83 kHz (but energy distributed fairly evenly throughout call), duration averages 2 ms (1-3 ms) (Kingston et al. 1999). Audible social calls comprising low frequency multiharmonic narrowband calls recorded from captive bats (Heller & Volleth 1989), possibly contact calls as emitted when individuals captured together were held separately.

Ecology: This species is mainly found in lowland forests with occasional individuals found in hill forests as well. Medway (1983) recorded specimens from lowland forests up to 600 m. The most common *Murina* in harp traps in KWR.

Breeding: One of the three females examined was pregnant in the month of December. KWR (lactating, pregnant): January (1,0), February (0,1), April (2,0), May (9,2), June (3,5), August (6,0), September (0,1), and October (0,1).

IUCN: LR (lc).

Distribution KWR (Site, individuals, recaptures): Jenderak Selatan: 45, 4; Kuala Gandah: 40, 6; Kuala Lompat: 74, 10; Kuala Serloh: 30, 7; Lubuk Baung: 36, 4. Notably more abundant at Kuala Lompat with 4.8% of individuals, elsewhere accounted for 1.5-2.5% of individuals. Also captured at Lembah Klau. DWNP specimens from Kuala Lompat and Sg. Chenderoh (Perlok).

Distribution: Java, Sumatra, Borneo, Peninsular Malaysia, and nearby islands.

Murina rozendaali Hill and Francis — Gilded Tube-nosed Bat
Kelawar Berselaput Kecil

Description: The fur on upperparts is banded, dark brown bases with some paler brown tips and many tips a shining golden brown, giving a general bronze or ochraceous-bronze colouration (Figure 3.105). Under-

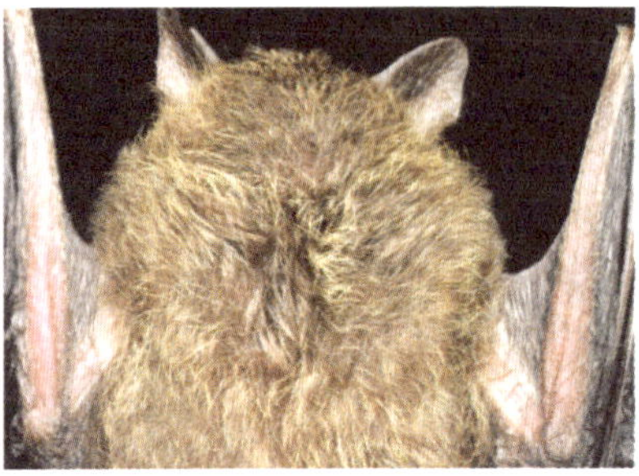

FIGURE 3.105 *Murina rozendaali,* face and underparts (left), dorsal (right) (Photos Kingston)

parts whitish with a slight buffy-yellow tinge in some individuals, particularly around the neck. Tibia is lightly furred as is the tail membrane (Figure 3.106). Wing membranes are brown. Ears are brown with pale bases. Some adult males (observed in at least three) have a large gland below the penis encompassing the scrotal area (Figure 3.107). The sides of the gland are pigmented but the surface is unpigmented and appears white. Structure is lightly haired and is covered in small white glands that extend halfway down the tail and that secrete a clear and pungent liquid. The gland can exceed approximately 14x9 mm at its widest. All other characteristics are similar to *M. aenea*, distinguished from it by the smaller size, and more yellow tinge to the underparts.

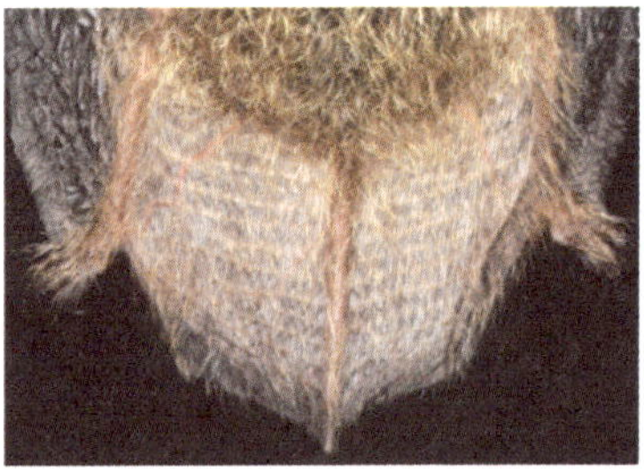

FIGURE 3.106 Furred tibia, feet, tail, and uropatagium of *Murina rozendaali* (Photo Kingston)

Measurements: (2 specimens) HB 43.0-45.0 mm, T 30.0-33.0 mm, FA 30.4-30.9 mm, E 12.5-13.0 mm, Wt 4.5 g. KWR: FA 28.2-31.8 mm (n = 6), Wt 4.5-5.0 g (n = 6).

Ecology: Specimens collected from Peninsular Malaysia all from primary forests.

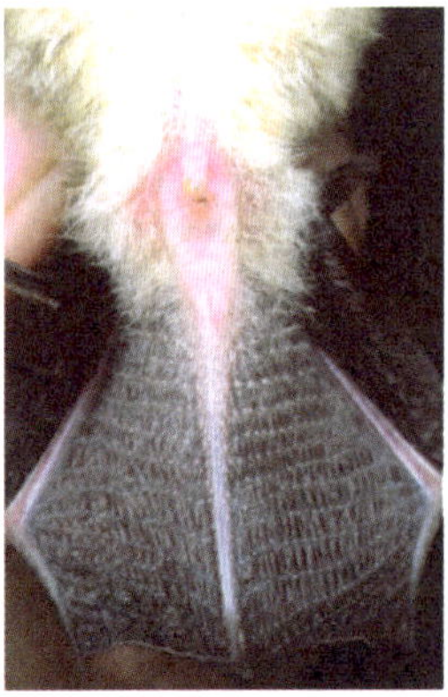

FIGURE 3.107 Ventral view of scrotal area of *Murina rozendaali* (Photo Kingston)

Breeding: Female lactating in June in KWR. Males with enlarged scrotal area captured in January.

IUCN: LR (nt).

Distribution KWR (Site, individuals, recaptures): Jenderak Selatan: 1, 0; Kuala Gandah: 3, 0; Kuala Serloh: 3, 0; Lubuk Baung: 1, 0. Also recorded at Kuala Lompat by Kingston et al. (2003), but rare at all sites (< 0.5%).

Distribution: Peninsular Malaysia, and Borneo.

Murina huttoni (Peters) — Hutton's Tube-nosed Bat
Kelawar Hidung-laras Bukit

Description: The colour of the hairs on the upperparts and underparts are similar to *M. cyclotis* from which it is distinguished by shorter forearm and longer ears.

Measurements: (4 specimens) HB 44.0-50.0 mm, T 36.0-40.0 mm, FA 32.0-36.0 mm, Tb 16.0-20.0 mm, E 16.5-17 mm, Wt 5.5-7.5 g.

Ecology: The four specimens were netted from lowland and hill forests. The first record of this species by Medway (1972) was from Gunung Benom at 1400 m.

Breeding: The only female examined was pregnant in May.

IUCN: LR (nt).

Distribution KWR: Known only from Medway's first record in hill forest at 1400 m up Gunung Benom.

Distribution: Tibet, NE and S China, NW India to Vietnam, Thailand, and Peninsular Malaysia.

Subfamily Kerivoulinae - Woolly or Funnel-eared Bats

There are 10 species in two genera (*Kerivoula* and *Phoniscus*) in Peninsular Malaysia, of which seven species have been recorded in Krau. The subfamily includes some of the smallest bats in the world, and they can be distinguished by distinct funnel-shaped ears with a large pointed tragus.

Kerivoula papillosa (Temminck) — Papillose Bat
Kelawar Hutan Besar

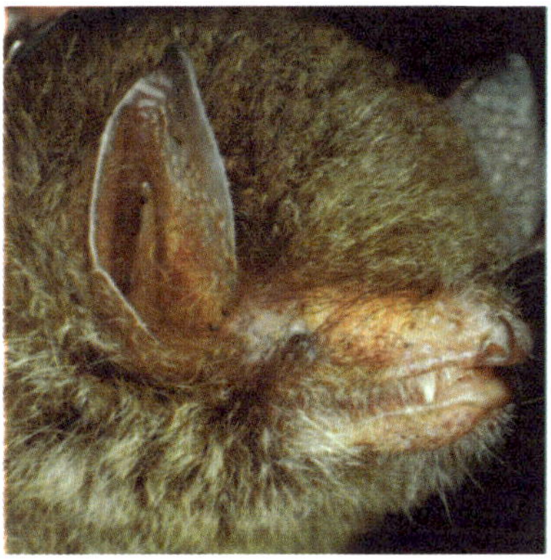

FIGURE 3.108 *Kerivoula papillosa* (Photo Kingston)

Description: Upperparts light brown to fawn, underparts paler. Fur is long and fluffy (Figure 3.108). Flight membrane brown. Ears funnel shaped. Tragus is long, slender and pointed. Distinguished from all other *Kerivoula* species by its large size.

Measurements: (5 specimens) HB 45.0-67.0 mm, T 35.0-57.0 mm, FA 41.0-44.0 mm, Tb 18.5-25.5 mm, E 14.0-16.0 mm, Wt 6.0-9.7.0 g. KWR: FA 36.8-47.0 mm (n = 514), Wt 6.0-12.8 g (n = 508).

Echolocation: High frequency, very broadband FM sweeps, of low intensity and short duration, and typically emitted in groups of 3-4 calls. Mean initial frequency 180 kHz, terminal frequency 73 kHz, peak frequency 93 kHz (but energy distributed fairly evenly throughout call), duration averages 2-3 ms (Kingston et al. 1999).

Ecology: Inhabits primary forests of all altitudes. Medway (1983) reported it roosting in pairs in dead and broken bamboo stems. In KWR roosting ecology was studied by radio-tracking 10 females and 12 males. The majority of roosts were hollows in small standing live trees with DBH 4-15 cm, and height < 20 m (Figure 3.109). Small entrances, rarely more than 3-5 cm wide or tall (Figure 3.110) opened between 0.5-10 m above the ground (most commonly < 5 m). Both males and females were found roosting solitarily and in mixed-sex groups of two to seven, although males were slightly more likely to be found roosting alone than females Although almost half the individuals remained faithful to the same roost for the duration of the transmitter life (up to eight days), many switched among two, three and on one occasion four roosts, and from roosting alone to roosting in a group. Roosts occupied for a single night tended to be more ephemeral or less stable structures (smaller, or more exposed hollows in dead trees, crevices, and foliage). Similar roosting ecology for this species has been observed in Sulawesi (T. Kingston and S. Rossiter, unpub. data).

FIGURE 3.109 *Kerivoula papillosa* roost tree, note small entrance c. 1 m above ground (Photo Fletcher)

Recapture rates are high, and many individuals are recaught repeatedly suggesting that the home range for this species is relatively small. The average distance travelled between captures for adults at Lubuk Baung was just 142 m for females (n = 100), and 160 m for males (n = 171). Preliminary radio-tracking studies further suggest that this species forages within a 100-300 m of the roost, resting at night roosts for part of the night.

FIGURE 3.110 *Kerivoula papillosa* roost entrance, with aerial of transmitter protruding (Photo Fletcher)

Breeding: One of the three females examined was pregnant in September. KWR: lactating and pregnant January (5, 0), February (6, 6), March (4, 15), April (6, 3) May (44, 9), June (24, 1), July (11, 8), August (6, 1), September (11, 0), and October (12,0).

IUCN: LR (lc)

Distribution KWR (Site, individuals, recaptures): Jenderak Selatan: 157, 97; Kuala Gandah: 136, 121; Kuala Lompat: 135, 105; Kuala Serloh: 124, 110; Lubuk Baung: 101, 108. Generally common, with relative abundance from 4.3% at Lubuk Baung to 10.4% at Kuala Serloh. Also captured at Lembah Klau.

Distribution: NE India, Thailand, Cambodia, Vietnam, Peninsular Malaysia, Sumatra, Java, Sulawesi, and Borneo.

Kerivoula intermedia Hill and Francis — Small Woolly Bat, Kelawar Kecil Berbulu

FIGURE 3.111 *Kerivoula intermedia* (Photo Kingston)

Description: Upperparts orange brown to rufous with dark, slatey-grey bases to hairs, underparts slightly paler (Figure 3.111). Wing membranes dark brown to blackish. Described as separate from *K. minuta* in Borneo, but this distinction is less certain in Peninsular Malaysia where there is extensive size overlap. Kingston et al. (2003a) split by forearm length and body weight, but subject to more detailed morphological and genetic analysis, all *intermedia*-like *Kerivoula* at Krau are currently allocated to *K. intermedia.*

Measurements: (15 specimens) HB 30.0-40.0 mm, T 24.0-42.0 mm, FA 26.7-31.3 mm, Tb 13.5-19.0 mm, E 11.0-13.5 mm, Wt 2.5-4.0 g. KWR: FA 24.2-33.3 mm (n = 1,387), Wt 2.0-5.5 g (n = 1,354).

Echolocation: High frequency, very broadband FM sweeps, of low intensity and short duration, and typically emitted in groups of 2-4 calls. Mean initial frequency 173 kHz, terminal frequency 77 kHz, peak frequency 101 kHz (but energy distributed fairly evenly throughout call), duration averages 2 ms (Kingston et al. 1999).

Ecology: This is an extremely common bat at Krau Wildlife Reserve, readily captured in harp traps but able to avoid mist nets. Consequently its abundance throughout the Peninsula has likely been greatly underestimated. Nothing is known of the roosting habit.

Breeding: KWR (lactating, pregnant): January (2,0), February (4,5), March (0,29), April (1,10), May (93, 12), June (27, 2), July (11,1), August (1, 14), September (5, 15), and October (9, 17).

IUCN: LR (nt).

Distribution KWR (Site, individuals, recaptures): Jenderak Selatan: 308, 106; Kuala Gandah: 338, 131; Kuala Lompat: 219, 92; Kuala Serloh: 260, 95; Lubuk Baung: 348, 91. The most abundant species at Kuala Serloh with 21.9% of individuals and consistently very common elsewhere with abundance ranging from 14.7% at Lubuk Baung to 17.8% at Kuala Gandah. Recapture rates were high, with females at Lubuk Baung travelling an average of 210 m (n = 13) between captures and males 150 m (n = 135). Also captured at Lembah Klau. DWNP specimen from Kuala Lompat.

Distribution: Borneo, and Peninsular Malaysia.

Kerivoula pellucida Waterhouse — Clear-winged Bat
Kelawar Kepak Jernih

FIGURE 3.112 *Kerivoula pellucida* (Photo Kingston)

Description: Fur long and fluffy, brown to fawn or grey with pale bases to the hairs (Figures 3.112 and 3.113). The underparts are whitish and the flight membrane is very pale greyish-brown to whitish and virtually translucent; it is possible to read print through the membrane. Face and ears often pinkish-yellow. Adult males have a swelling (presumably a gland) approximately two-thirds of the way down the tail.

Measurements: (7 specimens) HB 44.0-48.0 mm, T 41.0-47.0 mm, FA 29.8-32.0 mm, Tb

17.0-20.0 mm, E 13.0-16.0 mm, Wt 3.5-5.5 g. KWR: FA 28.1-34.0 mm (n = 588), Wt 3.5-6.0 g (n = 564).

Echolocation: High frequency, very broadband FM sweeps, of low intensity and short duration, and typically emitted in groups of 2-8 calls and at the highest pulse repetition rate of any of the *Kerivoula* recorded. Mean initial frequency 178 kHz, terminal frequency 58 kHz, mean peak frequency 96 kHz (but energy distributed fairly evenly throughout call). Duration averages 2-3 ms (Kingston et al. 1999). The species also produces low frequency, intense multi-harmonic calls with a terminal upsweep which can be integrated into the FM orientation sequence, and these maybe contact calls (Kingston et al. 2000b).

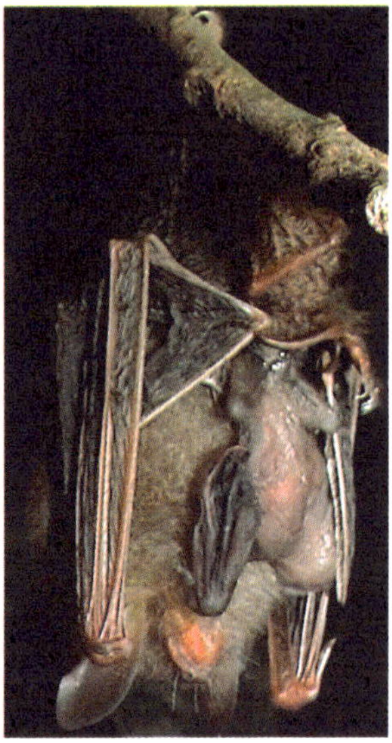

FIGURE 3.113 *Kerivoula pellucida* and newborn pup (Photo Elder)

Ecology: Relatively common in the understorey of KWR, but rarely captured in mist nets. Payne and Francis (1985) reported it roosting in dead curled banana leaves and foraging in the upperstorey of tall forests, but in KWR an individual followed on release roosted in a cluster of dead leaves in the understorey with conspecifics. Individuals captured in harp traps frequently roost in tight clusters, suggestive of social bonds. This is the most manoeuvrable of all the *Kerivoula* at KWR, and in flight trials can pass through openings as small as 10 cm wide without touching obstacles (T. Kingston, unpub. data); it is therefore predicted to forage or roost in dense vegetation. Note that the wing membrane is fragile and this species should not be banded.

Breeding: KWR (lactating, pregnant): January (3, 2), February (0, 2), March (6, 7), April (10, 3), May (54, 1), June (27, 3), July (22, 0), August (11, 9), September (13, 1), and October (4, 5) (Figure 113).

IUCN: LR(lc).

Distribution KWR (Site, individuals and recaptures pooled): Jenderak Selatan: 174; Kuala Gandah: 81; Kuala Lompat: 184; Kuala Serloh: 121;

Lubuk Baung: 115. As this species cannot be banded, it is not possible to distinguish between captures and recaptures. A common species at all sites, with abundance ranging from 4.3% at Kuala Gandah to 10.1% at Kuala Serloh and 11.9% at Kuala Lompat where it was the third most common bat. Also captured at Lembah Klau.

Distribution: Borneo, Philippines, Java and Sumatra, and Peninsular Malaysia.

Kerivoula sp.

FIGURE 3.114 *Kerivoula* sp. (Photo Kingston)

Description: Approximately the same size as *K. intermedia* but clearly distinguished by pelage, which is brown on the upperparts with light-brown to golden tips (Figures 3.114 and 3.115). Underparts white-buffy. Description for this species is in preparation (Francis et al. in prep).

Measurements: (2 specimens) HB 37.0-40.0 mm, T 35.0 mm, FA 28.2-29.1 mm, Tb 14.0 mm, E 11.0 mm, Wt 2.5 g. KWR: FA 29.2-33.3 mm (n = 29), Wt 2.0-4.0 g (n = 29).

Echolocation: High frequency, very broadband FM sweeps, of low intensity and short duration, and typically emitted in groups of 2-8 calls. Mean initial frequency 173 kHz, terminal frequency 50 kHz, peak frequency 99 kHz (but energy distributed fairly evenly

FIGURE 3.115 Ventral view of *Kerivoula* sp. (Photo Kingston)

throughout call), duration averages 2-3 ms (Kingston et al. 1999).

Ecology: Known only from the rainforest understorey of KWR, where it is occasionally captured in harp traps.

Breeding: KWR (lactating, pregnant): February (0, 1), April (2, 1), May (1, 0), June (1, 0), and September (1, 0).

Distribution KWR: (Site, individuals, recaptures): Jenderak Selatan: 4, 0; Kuala Gandah: 4, 1; Kuala Lompat: 9, 2; Kuala Serloh: 13, 2; Lubuk Baung: 3, 0. Present but rare at all sites (relative abundance 0.1-1.1%).

Distribution: KWR, Peninsular Malaysia.

Phoniscus jagorii (Peters) — Peter's Trumpet Eared Bat, Kelawar Putih Di-telinga

Description: Hairs on the upperparts with up to four bands (brown, buff, brown, golden-yellow) the outermost commonly a buffy-gold colour giving a frosted appearance (Figures 3.116 and 3.117). Wrists, finger and forearm also flecked with short buffy-gold hairs. Differs from *Kerivoula* in that the tragus is notched at the base of the posterior margin (Figure 3.118), and the canine is grooved. Differs from *P. atrox* by larger size.

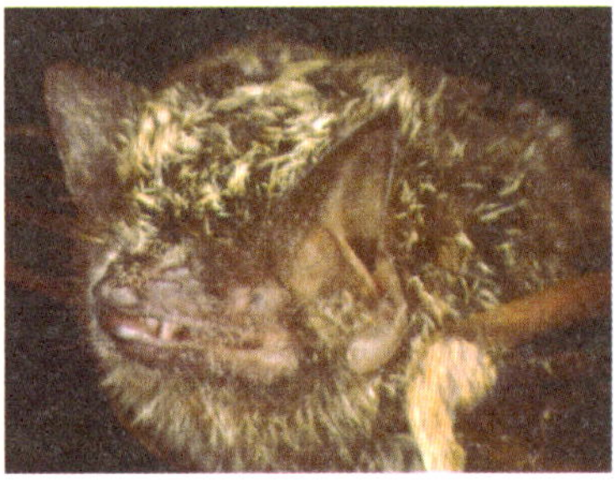

FIGURE 3.116 *Phoniscus jagorii* (Photo Kingston)

Measurement: 1 specimen and 3 individuals. HB 53.0 mm, T 51.0 mm, FA 39.0-42.5 mm, E 17.0 mm, Wt 9.0-11.0 g.

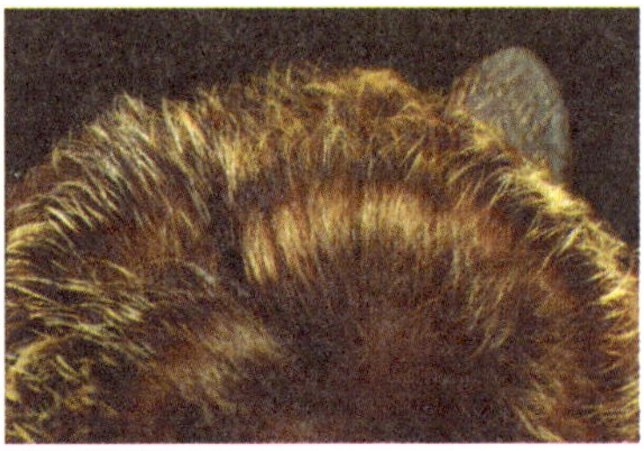

FIGURE 3.117 Dorsal fur of *Phoniscus jagorii* parted to show banding (Photo Kingston)

Echolocation: High frequency, very broadband FM sweeps, of low intensity and short duration, and typically emitted in groups of 2-7 calls. Mean initial frequency 169 kHz, terminal frequency 70 kHz, peak frequency 94 kHz (but energy distributed fairly evenly throughout call), duration 2 ms (Kingston et al. 1999).

Ecology: First record came from harp-trapping in primary forest at KWR (Kingston et al. 1997), but this bat is rare in the understorey.

IUCN: LR (lc).

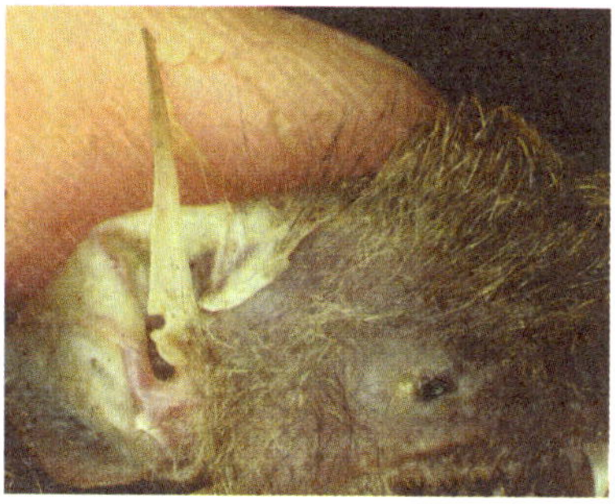

FIGURE 3.118 Unpigmented tragus of *Phoniscus jagorii* with notch near base (Photo Kingston)

Distribution KWR: Two records at Kuala Lompat (with an additional three reported in Kingston et al. (2003a)), and one record from Jenderak Selatan in May 2005. DWNP specimen from Kuala Lompat.

Distribution: Laos, Peninsular Malaysia, Borneo, Java, Bali, Sulawesi, Lesser Sunda Islands, and Samar Island.

Phoniscus atrox Miller

Gilded Groove-toothed Bat
Kelawar Putih Di-telinga

FIGURE 3.119 *Phoniscus atrox* (Photo Kingston)

Description: The hairs are soft and fluffy, upperparts tricoloured: light brown or grey at the base, followed by a buffy band then brown or black with golden or buff tips, which are especially pronounced on the head (Figure 3.119). The overall appearance is golden brown and black. Underparts paler with fewer gold flecks, but thumbs, edge of the blackish/brown wing, forearm, legs, tail and feet are thinly covered with fine hairs of gold. The unpigmented-whitish pointed tragus contrasts with the brownish ears. All individuals have a distinctive acrid smell. Similar to *P. jagorii* in features but distinguished from it by smaller size.

Measurements: (3 specimens) HB 40.0-41.0 mm, T 35.0-41.0 mm, FA 35.0-35.5 mm, Tb 14-5.0-16.5 mm, E 13.0-15.0 mm, Wt 5.4-5.9 g. KWR: FA 29.2-35.9 mm, Wt 3.0-6.5 g (n = 72).

Echolocation: High frequency, very broadband FM sweeps, of low intensity and short duration, and typically emitted in groups of 2-3 calls. Mean initial frequency 166 kHz, terminal frequency 60 kHz, peak frequency 87 kHz (but energy distributed fairly evenly throughout call), duration c. 3 ms (Kingston et al. 1999).

Ecology: Captured in harp traps in primary forest, although patchily distributed. In KWR, one individual found roosting in an abandoned suspended bird's nest, and this habit has been reported in Australia for *Phoniscus papuensis* (Schulz 2000).

Breeding: One of the two females examined was pregnant in August. KWR: lactating Jan (1), May (1), Jun (3), Oct (1); pregnant April (1), and October (3).

IUCN: LR (lc).

Distribution KWR (Site, individuals, recaptures): Jenderak Selatan: 12, 6; Kuala Gandah: 15, 3; Kuala Lompat: 20, 13; Kuala Serloh: 16, 5; Lubuk Baung: 16, 4. A relatively rare bat with abundance less than 1%, except at Kuala Serloh and Kuala Lompat where they comprised 1.3% of individuals. Recapture rates are generally high, from 20-65%. DWNP specimen from Kuala Lompat.

Distribution: S Thailand, Peninsular Malaysia, Sumatra, and Borneo.

Subfamily Vespertilioninae

This is the largest subfamily consisting of 8 genera with approximately 23 species in Peninsular Malaysia, 14 of which have been found in the reserve. Members of this family lack the distinguishing features of the other three subfamilies and have simple muzzles, normal wings and well-developed but rounded ears. The tragus is either straight or slightly curved.

Hesperoptenus blanfordi (Dobson)

Blanford's Bat
(Lesser False Serotine)
Kelawar Petang Palsu Kecil

Description: Fur sleek with a glossy sheen to it. General colour dark brown with reddish tinge, underparts slightly paler. Flight membrane brown. Thickened dark brown pads on base of thumb and sole of foot. Pads are slightly kidney-shaped. Distinguished by size which is intermediate between *H. tomesi* and *H. doriae*.

Measurements: (2 specimens) HB 37.0-45.0 mm, T 33.0-34.0 mm, FA 31.0-36.0 mm, Tb 13.4-14.0 mm, E 11.0-12.0 mm, Wt 3.6-5.5 g. KWR: FA 25.3-26.8 mm (n = 10), Wt 5.5-7.5 g (n = 8).

Echolocation: Narrowband calls that alternate in peak frequency when the bat is flying above 10 m. High frequency calls start at a mean frequency of 60 kHz and end at c. 40 kHz, with mean peak frequency of 44 kHz and duration 6.6 ms. Low frequency calls start at 55 kHz, end at 33 kHz with peak of 36 kHz and duration 8.3 ms (Kingston et al. 2003b).

Ecology: Found roosting in small colonies (less than 10 individuals) in the entrance of limestone caves and also in hill forests. At KWR, recorded foraging in open spaces and tree-fall gaps, and above rivers. Captured in mist nets over rivers.

Breeding: One female examined was pregnant with a single embryo in January.

IUCN: LR (lc).

Distribution KWR: 9 captured in harp traps at Kuala Lompat, and a 10th in a mist net set over the Lompat River (Kingston et al. 2003a).

Distribution: Myanmar, Thailand, Cambodia, Laos, Peninsular Malaysia, and Borneo.

Tylonycteris robustula Thomas

Greater Bamboo Bat
Kelawar Buluh Besar

Description: The fur is smooth, sleek and uniformly brown on both the upper and underparts. Flight membrane dark brown. The distinguishing characteristic of this bat is its flattened head (Figure 3.120) and body together with disc-liked pads that are circular in shape at the wrist and on the soles of the hind feet (Figure 3.121). Differs from *T. pachypus* by larger size.

FIGURE 3.120 *Tylonycteris robustula* (Photo Kingston)

Measurements: (106 specimens) HB 44.0-55.0 mm, T 28.0-34.0 mm, FA 28.0-33.0 mm, Tb 12.0-14.0 mm, E 8.0-12.0 mm, Wt 6.5-10.5 g.

Echolocation: Frequency-modulated sweeps of 2.0-8.5 ms starting between 90-100 kHz and ending in a constant frequency component which varies in frequency depending upon the length of the call; 48 kHz in short calls, 40 kHz in long calls and 35 kHz in very long calls (Heller 1989). Start frequency recorded for this species by T. Wood (per. com.) was much lower, with an average of 49 kHz (3 bats, 62 calls individuals, flying 5-10 m above ground).

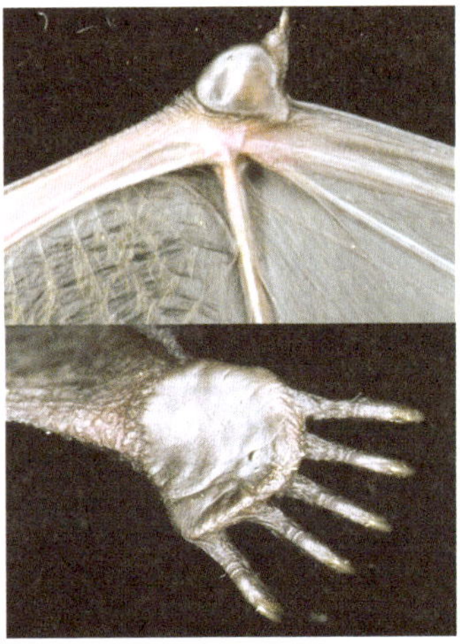

FIGURE 3.121 Pads on wrist (top) and foot (bottom) of *T. robustula* (Photo Kingston)

Ecology: The species roosts in the internodal space (culm) of standing bamboo, and appears to show a preference for the large bamboo *Gigantochloa scortechinii* (Marshall 1971). It gains access through holes made by the larvae of chrysomelid beetles (*Lasyochila gori*) when they emerge from pupation inside the culm. The roost entrances examined by Marshall (1971) were approximately 4-8 mm wide and 29-81 mm long. These are small holes, and the bats have flattened skulls to squeeze through, and suction pads on their wrists and ankles to grip the smooth surface inside the culm (Medway and Marshall, 1972) (Figure 3.121). In a survey of 193 occupied roosts, Marshall (1971) found that 41% were occupied by a single male, 21% by one male and one or more females, 6% by multi-male groups, 9% by single females and 10% by multi-female groups. Groups may reach 60 individuals. Being associated with bamboo in forested areas, this bat is commonly found in lowland forest, although they are occasionally netted in hill forest. The biology and ecology of this bat and *T. pachypus* was studied in depth by Medway (1972).

Breeding: Twenty-three of 60 females examined were pregnant. January (4 specimens), April (1), May (1), Oct (9), November (5) and December (3). Of these 14 individuals were found with twin embryos with the remaining nine with a single embryo. Medway (1983) reported that two young were normally born at a time.

IUCN: LR (lc).

Distribution KWR: A single individual was captured in a harp trap at Kuala Serloh, and another captured in mist nets over the Lompat River at Kuala Lompat (T. Wood unpub. data). Also recorded at Kuala Lompat by (Zubaid 1993). DWNP specimens from Kuala Lompat.

Distribution: NE India, Myanmar, Cambodia, Laos, Vietnam, S China to the Philippines, Sulawesi, Sumatra, Java, Bali, and Borneo.

Tylonycteris pachypus (Temminck) Lesser Flat-headed Bat
Kelawar Buluh Kecil

Description: Upperparts brown to chestnut-brown, with bases a paler brown. Fur on underparts is paler, but light ginger-chestnut. The muzzle is without fur and the skin is dark brown/black as are the ears and flight membrane. The penis is slightly club-shaped with a circular fleshy tip. All other characters being identical to the *T. robustula*, differing only by being smaller in size.

Measurements: (63 specimens) HB 34.0-42.0 mm, T 24.0-31.0 mm, FA 24.0-28.0 mm, Tb 7.0-13.0 mm, E 8.0-11.0 mm, Wt 3.0-4.8 g.

Echolocation: Frequency-modulated sweeps of 2-7 ms starting at c. 125 kHz and ending in a constant frequency component which varies in frequency depending upon the length of the call; 58 kHz in short calls, 50 kHz in long calls (Heller 1989). Start frequency recorded for this species by T. Wood (per. com.) was much lower, with an average of 60 kHz (8 bats, 232 calls, flying 5-10 m above ground).

Ecology: Similar to *T. robustula*, although gregarious, the species does not roost in large numbers. The roost entrances examined by Marshall (1971) were approximately 4-7 mm wide and 23-64 mm long. In a survey of 208 occupied roosts, he found that 30% were occupied by a single male, 22% by one male and one or more females, 10% by multi-male groups, 5% by single females and 13% by multi-female groups. Both species were often found in the same roost, but typically *T. pachypus* uses roosts with smaller access holes (Medway & Marshall 1972). Inside the culm, both *Tylonycteris* species are parasitized by an insect ectoparasite *Basilia hispida* (Diptera: Nycteribiidae). The adult flies deposit prepupae within the bamboo internode and adult parasites are stimulated to emerge from the pupal instar stage after about 25 days by the presence of the host bat (Marshall 1971). They readily live and reproduce on both *T. pachypus* and *T. robustula* but Marshall (1971) suggested that *T. pachypus* may be the main host as infestation levels were higher. The flies distribute themselves in areas that are difficult for the bat to groom when it is roosting (between the shoulder blades, under the chin, in the arm pits) and gravitate to the tail, urogenital openings and back during flight.

Breeding: Seventeen of 25 pregnant females were examined. April (6 specimens), May (3), Sept (5), November (1), and December (2), of which 13 of these pregnant females were found with twin embryos. Marshall (1971) reported that both *Tylonycteris* spp. were highly seasonal breeders, mating in October-November and giving birth to twin offspring in mid-April each year.

IUCN: LR (lc).

Distribution in KWR: Captured in mist nets over the Lompat River at Kuala Lompat (T. Wood unpub. data) and recorded at Kuala Lompat by Zubaid (1993).

Distribution: Bangladesh, India, Myanmar, S China, Thailand, Myanmar, Laos, Cambodia, Vietnam to Peninsular Malaysia, Philippines, Sumatra, Java, Borneo, Bali (Indonesia), and Andaman Islands.

Glischropus tylopus (Dobson) — Common Thick-thumbed Bat
Kelawar Tapak Tangan Putih

FIGURE 3.122 *Glischropus tylopus* (Photo Juliana)

Description: Upperparts dark brown to blackish with underparts paler. The flight membrane and ears are dark grey (Figure 3.122). The most distinctive features are the unpigmented kidney-shaped pads at the base of the thumb and sole of the foot. Differs from *Tylonycteris* by the shape of the pads (circular and longer in *Tylonycteris*) and head and body not flattened (flattened in *Tylonycteris*).

Measurements: (19 specimens) HB 36.0-46.0 mm, T 32.0-39.0 mm, FA 26.0-32.5 mm, Tb 13.0-15.0 mm, E 8.0-11.0 mm, Wt 3.8-7.5 g. KWR: FA 29.8-30.1 mm, Wt 4.5-5.0 g (n = 4).

Echolocation: Steep FM sweeps starting at about 95 kHz with the peak of the CF component between 45 and 49 kHz, duration 3-7 ms (Heller 1989).

Ecology: Primarily a forest species, inhabiting mainly lowland forest but also found in hill forest. Frequently found roosting in small groups in bamboo stems or dead or damaged bamboo (Kofron 1994). Occasionally found roosting together with *Tylonycteris*.

Breeding: Four of the eight females were found pregnant with a single embryo each in the months of June, July, and November.

IUCN: LR (lc).

Distribution in KWR: Kingston et al. (2003a) reported two captured in harp traps at Kuala Lompat, two in mist nets set over the Lompat River, and a third caught in a flick net near the rest house.

Distribution: Myanmar, Thailand, Peninsular Malaysia, Borneo, Palawan (Philippines), Sumatra and N Molucca Islands.

Pipistrellus javanicus (Gray) Javan Pipistrelle
Kelawar Hidung Pendek Java

Description: Fur on upperparts dark brown, underparts paler (Figure 3.123). The first premolar is small and displaced inwards from the toothrow.

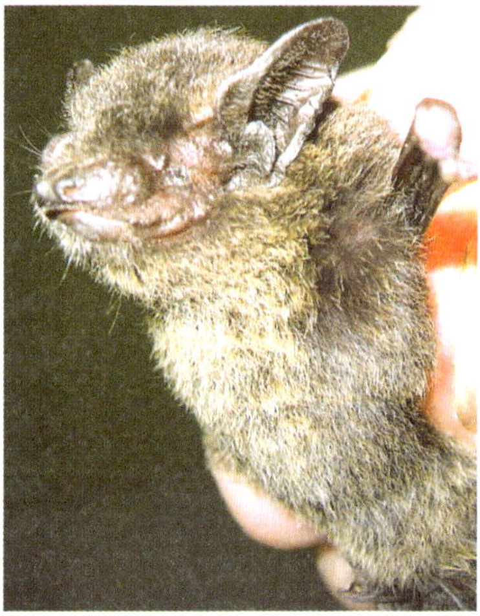

FIGURE 3.123 *Pipistrellus javanicus* (Photo Wood)

Measurements: (9 specimens) HB 40.0-45.0 mm, T 32.0-35.0 mm, FA 31.0-35.0 mm, Tb 12.0-14.0 mm, E 9.0-12.0 mm, Wt 5.0-6.5 g.

Echolocation: Calls of a single individual flying 2-5 m above ground were frequency-modulated sweeps of average duration 5.4 ms, starting at 54 kHz and ending in a constant frequency component with a peak frequency of 39 kHz and end frequency 37 kHz (17 calls) (T. Wood unpub. data).

Ecology: The specimens were collected from mangrove, hill and lowland forest. Medway (1983) recorded from towns and forest.

Breeding: One of the two females examined was pregnant with a single embryo in April.

IUCN: LR (lc).

Distribution in KWR: Recorded at Kuala Lompat by Zubaid (1993).

Distribution: E Afghanistan, N Pakistan, N and C India, SE Tibet, Myanmar, Thailand, Vietnam, through SE Asia to Lesser Sunda Islands and the Philippines.

Pipistrellus stenopterus (Dobson) Narrow-winged Pipistrelle
Kelawar Malam Kecil

Description: Uniformly reddish brown. Distinguished from all other *Pipistrellus* by the length of the 5th metacarpal which is much shorter than the 4th metacarpal creating a narrow wing. It is also the largest of the *Pipistrellus*.

Measurements: (16 specimens) HB 55.0-60.0 mm, T 55.0-57.0 mm, FA 39.0-42.0 mm, Tb 18.0-22.0 mm, E 14.0-16.0 mm, Wt 18.0-22.0 g. KWR: FA 37.3-40.9 mm (n = 7), Wt 14.3-20.5 g (n = 4).

Echolocation: Narrowband calls that alternate in peak frequency when the bat is flying higher than 10 m above the ground. High-frequency calls start at a mean frequency of 56 kHz and end at c. 33 kHz, with mean peak frequency of 37 kHz and duration 9.7 ms. Low-frequency calls start at 43 kHz, end at 28 kHz with peak of 31 kHz and duration 13.8 ms (Kingston et al. 2003b).

Ecology: Gregarious, roosting in hollow trees in forest and plantations particularly rubber trees. Also found on roofs of houses in rural areas. Occasionally found roosting with *Scotophilus kuhlii* in roofs of houses in urban and rural areas. Typically forages in open spaces and over rivers - captured in KWR in mist nets set over slow-moving rivers.

Breeding: Four of the seven females examined were pregnant. March (1 specimen), June (2), and July (1). Two of the pregnant females were found with twin embryos, with the remaining a single embryo.

IUCN: LR (lc).

Distribution in KWR: 7 individuals captured in mist nets set over the Lompat River at Kuala Lompat (Kingston et al. 2003a). DWNP specimens from Kuala Lompat.

Distribution: Peninsular Malaysia, Sumatra, Riau Arch., N Borneo, and Mindanao (Philippines).

Arielulus societatis (Hill) (formerly *Pipistrellus societatis*)

Social Pipistrelle
Kelawar Benom

Description: Hairs on the upperparts very dark brown to black and tipped with orange or gold (Figure 3.124), underparts browner tipped with grey. Wing membrane is uniformly black. In appearance resembles *A. circumdatus*, distinguished by smaller size and length of maxillary toothrow being 5.1-5.3 mm compared with 5.7-6.5 mm in the latter.

FIGURE 3.124 *Arielulus societus* (Photo Juliana)

Measurements: (2 specimens) HB 41.0-44.0 mm, T 33.0-37.0mm, FA 35.0-39.0 mm, Tb 14.5-15 mm, E 8.5-9 mm, Wt 4.3-5.5 g.

Ecology: Both the specimens were collected from primary lowland and hill forests. Medway collected the first specimen in 1972 in disturbed secondary forest on the northeast slope of Gunung Benom (Base Camp (03°51'N, 102°11'E), 266 m). In Selangor, found roosting in a tree trunk hole beside a forest stream.

IUCN: DD

Distribution in KWR: Known only from the specimen collected on the northeast slope of Gunung Benom.

Distribution: Peninsular Malaysia.

Myotis ridleyi Thomas

Ridley's Myotis
Kelawar Tikus Telinga Kecil

Description: Upperparts uniformly dark brown with short velvety fur. Underparts slightly paler, grey brown to dark brown. Face and muzzle brown, wings brown-black; ears brown black with tragus curved forward. Feet small, wing membrane joins foot at base of toes. Distinguished from all other *Myotis* species by having 5 upper and 5 lower cheek teeth (only 2 premolars), contrasting with 6 and 6 in all other species. A thick-set "chunky" bat for its size.

Measurement: (4 specimens): HB 36.0-41.0 mm, T 23.0-33.0 mm, FA 29.3-30.0 mm, Tb 12.0-13.0 mm, E 8.0-11.0 mm, Wt 4.2-4.7 g. KWR: FA 27.0-37.0 mm (n = 96), Wt 4.0-6.5 g (n = 95).

Ecology: The species is found in primary forest and in caves far from the forest (Medway 1983). Although it is generally an uncommon species, it is one of the few *Myotis* species captured in harp traps set in the forest understorey, suggesting it may be more adapted to foraging in the forest interior than is typical for *Myotis*.

Breeding: One of the two female specimens was pregnant with a single embryo in April. KWR: lactating - May (4), August (1), October (2), pregnant - March (1), and October (1).

IUCN: LR (nt).

Distribution KWR (Site, individuals, recaptures): Jenderak Selatan: 1, 0; Kuala Gandah: 13, 0; Kuala Lompat: 25, 1; Kuala Serloh: 5, 0; Lubuk Baung: 8, 0. A relatively rare bat to capture in the forest understorey, although abundance at Kuala Lompat reached 1.6%.

Distribution: Peninsular Malaysia, and Borneo.

Myotis muricola (Gray) Nepalese Whiskered Bat
Kelawar Daun Pisang

Description: Upperparts dark brown or greyish brown to blackish, underparts buffy grey to blackish (Figure 3.125). Flight membrane blackish. Second premolar small and slightly intruded from the tooth row. The species *Myotis mystacinus* was reported by Medway (1983), however Corbet and Hill (1992) reported that *M. mystacinus* is not within the range of Malaysia and reclassified the species found in Peninsular Malaysia as *M. muricola* (Simmons in press). Slightly smaller than *M. ater*

FIGURE 3.125 *Myotis muricola* (Photo Kingston)

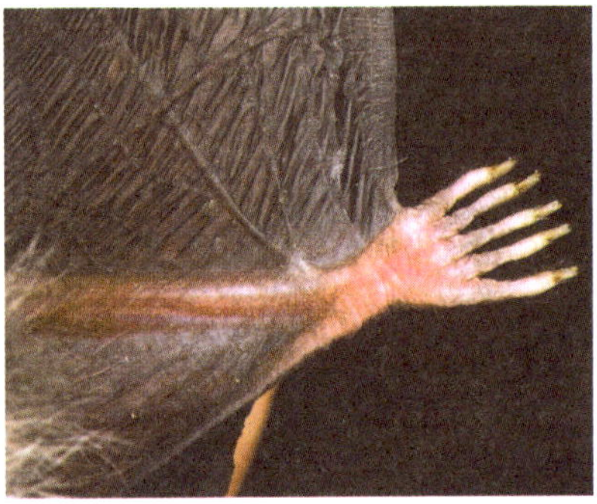

FIGURE 3.126 Ventral view of left foot of *Myotis muricola* to show attachment of wing membrane (Photo Kingston)

with the 2nd upper premolar inline with the tooth row (rather than displaced inward as in *M. ater*) and canines longer than premolars. As for other species in the subgenus *Selysius*, wing membrane attached no more than 1 mm up from base of toes (Figure 3.126).

Measurements: (47 specimens) HB 39.0-43.0 mm, T 34.0-42.0 mm, FA 28.0-36.0 mm, Tb 13.0-16.0 mm, E 11.0-12.0 mm, Wt 3.0-5.0 g.

Ecology: The species is common in forested areas at all elevations and also in plantations where there are banana trees. It roosts in small groups of one to ten individuals in the tightly rolled central leaf of both wild and cultivated banana plants. They also occasionally roost at the entrance of caves that are covered by vegetation.

Breeding: Among the 27 females examined, 10 were found pregnant, October (2 specimens), January (3), March (3), and December (2). Twin embryos were found in 3 females with the remaining having a single embryo each. Medway (1983) reported that the species bred all year round.

IUCN: LR (lc)

Distribution in KWR: Two individuals were captured at Kuala Lompat (although Kingston et al. (2003a) report a further eight), and two at Lubuk

Baung. A rare capture in the forest understorey as this species tends to forage in tree-fall gaps and at the edge of vegetation.

Distribution: Afghanistan through N India and Nepal to Taiwan, Vietnam, Peninsular Malaysia, Indonesia, and New Guinea.

Myotis ater (Peters)

Peters's Myotis
Kelawar Peter

FIGURE 3.127 *Myotis ater* (Photo Juliana)

Description: Dark upperparts with slightly glossy tips, paler underparts with long black bases and buffy brown tips (Figure 3.127). Slightly larger than *M. muricola* with posterior upper premolar as long as canine and 2nd upper premolar very small and displaced inwards. Formerly included in *muricola*.

Measurements: FA 34.0-39.0 mm; Wt 5.0-8.0 g.

Ecology: Occasionally captured in harp traps in primary forest. Payne and Francis (1985) report it roosting individually or in small colonies in caves.

IUCN: LR (lc).

Distribution in KWR: Kuala Lompat: 5, 1; Kuala Serloh: 4, 0. A rare capture in the forest understorey as this species tends to forage in more open areas such as tree-fall gaps, midstorey openings and at the forest edge. An additional individual was captured in a flick net at Kuala Gandah.

Distribution: Vietnam, W Sumatra, Peninsular Malaysia, Sulawesi, Togian Island, N Borneo, Moluccas, Papua New Guinea, possibly the Philippines, and Australia.

Myotis siligorensis (Horsfield)

Himalayan Whiskered Bat
Kelawar Kumis Gua

Description: The upperparts are grey to dark brown or reddish-brown, underparts light buff (Figure 3.128). General appearance similar to *M. muricola*; distinguished by its smaller size and colouration, and from *M. ridleyi* by smaller size and presence of three premolars.

Measurements: (3 specimens) HB 33.0-35.0 mm, T 28.0-30.0 mm, FA 30.0-31.5 mm, Tb 12.0-13.0 mm, E 8.0-9.0 mm, Wt 2.9-3.3 g. KWR: FA 28.0-31.6 mm, Wt 2.8-3.3 g (n = 3).

FIGURE 3.128 *Myotis siligorensis* (Photo Wood)

Echolocation: Produces 5.4 ms long CF search signals at 66 kHz. The repetition rate is around 13 Hz. In the approach phase an initial broadband FM sweep was added. The buzz consisted of two phases, buzz I and buzz II. Buzz II was characterised by calls of short duration (around 0.3 ms), a constant high repetition rate (185 Hz), a distinct drop in frequency, and a prominent second harmonic (Surlykke et al. 1993).

Ecology: The specimens were collected from lowland and hill forests in Selangor and Pahang. Medway (1983) reported that this bat was found roosting in small groups in crevices of rocks and also in caves. At KWR captured and recorded acoustically, foraging around street lights at Kuala Lompat Field Station at the forest edge, and Surlykke et al. (1993) report it foraging in open spaces.

Breeding: The only female examined was pregnant in January.

IUCN: LR (lc).

Distribution in KWR: A single individual was captured in a harp trap at Kuala Lompat, with two further individuals captured in mist nets and a fourth taken with a hand net as it foraged around a street light at Kuala Lompat (Kingston et al. 2003a; T. Wood unpub. data).

Distribution: N India to S China, Myanmar, Vietnam, Laos, south to Peninsular Malaysia and Borneo.

Myotis horsfieldii (Temminck) — Horsfield's Myotis
Kelawar Lobang Batu

Description: Upperparts greyish brown, underparts grey to dark grey. Flight membrane dark grey. Distinguished from all other big-footed *Myotis* by the posterior margin of the wing membrane joining the foot midway between the ankle and the base of the outer toe.

Measurements: (45 specimens) HB 44.0-48.0 mm, T 37.0-40.0 mm, FA 34.0-39.0 mm, Tb 15.0-17.0 mm, E 13.0-17.0 mm, Wt 5.0-7.5 g

Echolocation: Steeply frequency-modulated calls without any CF component. Average duration of 27 calls of a single individual foraging over the Lompat River at Lubuk Baung was 1.8 ms with calls starting at 71 kHz and ending at 41 kHz (T. Wood unpub. data).

Ecology: Primarily a forest species of lowland and hill forests. In Pulau Langkawi, found roosting in limestone caves. Elsewhere are gregarious, roosting in small (2-5) to medium-sized groups in crevices of large rocks and boulders not far from forest streams, over which they forage. They are thought to be foraging by skimming insects from the water surface.

Breeding: Seventeen females of 26 females were found pregnant in January (4 specimens), March (2), April (4), May (2), June (1), and October (4). Two of the pregnant females were found with twin embryos. Lim (1967) recorded gravid females most months of the year with dependent young more often found in March to May.

IUCN: LR (lc).

Distribution in KWR: Captured in a mist net set over the Lompat River at Kuala Lompat (Kingston et al. 2003a; T. Wood unpub. data), and in mist nets over the Rivers Teris (Kuala Gandah) and Lompat (Lubuk Baung and Kuala Serloh) (T. Wood unpub. data). DWNP specimen from Kuala Lompat.

Distribution: India (including Andaman Islands), SE China, Thailand, Myanmar, Laos, Vietnam, Peninsular Malaysia, Java, Bali, Sulawesi, Borneo, and Philippines.

Myotis hasseltii (Temminck) — Lesser Large-footed Myotis
Kelawar Bakau

Description: Upperparts grey to pale brown, underparts greyish. The ears and wing membrane are pale brown giving a general greyish-brown appearance. Feet large with wing membrane attached at the ankle. The second upper premolar is displaced inwards and is very small. Distinguished from *M. adversus* which has longer fur and a larger upper premolar which is nearly in line with the toothrow, and from *M. horsfieldii* in which the wing membrane is attached to the side of the foot.

Measurements: (47 specimens) HB 44.0-60.0 mm, T 38.0-46.0 mm, FA 38.0-42.0 mm, Tb 17.0-20.0 mm, E 13.0-16.0 mm, Wt 8.0-11.0 g. KWR: FA 34.0-36.9 mm, Wt 7.0-7.8 g (n = 2).

Echolocation: Steeply frequency-modulated calls without any CF component. Duration 2.5-5.5 ms, starting at 82-104 kHz and sweeping down to 23-30 kHz. A second harmonic is regularly included (Heller 1989).

Ecology: Similar to *M. horsfieldii* and *M. adversus*. Forages close to the water surface, and is presumed to glean insects from the surface, or possibly take small fish from beneath the surface (unconfirmed). Elsewhere, primarily an inhabitant of coastal and mangrove forests. Gregarious, roosting in large numbers in crevices of rocks. In Pulau Langkawi, they were found roosting in limestone caves. Medway (1983) recorded a large colony of 25 bats in crack of large boulders offshore, isolated at high tide, at Pulau Langkawi.

Breeding: Thirteen of the 27 females examined were pregnant. January (9 specimens), February (2), and March (2). Medway (1983) found females either lactating or in advanced pregnancy in January with a single female dissected carrying a single foetus.

IUCN: LR (lc).

Distribution in KWR: Two individuals captured in mist nets set over the Lompat River at Kuala Lompat (Kingston et al. 2003a), and at Jenderak Selatan in a river mist net (T. Wood unpub. data).

Distribution: E India, Sri Lanka, Myanmar, Thailand, Cambodia, Vietnam, Peninsular Malaysia, Sumatra, Mentawai Islands, Riau Archipelago, Java, and Borneo.

Scotophilus kuhlii Leach — Lesser Asiatic Yellow House Bat
Kelawar Rumah

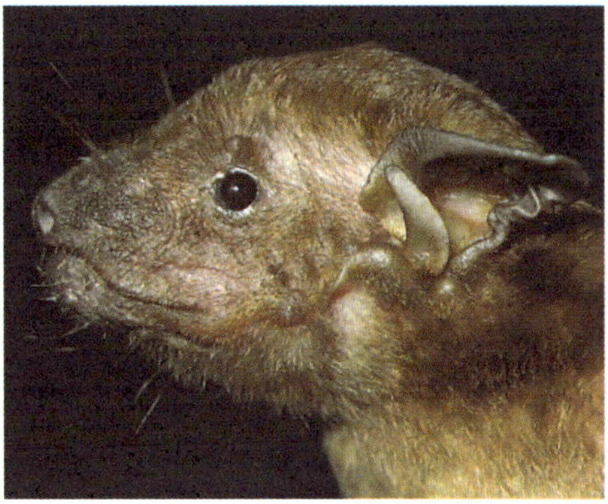

FIGURE 3.129 *Scotophilus kuhlii*. Note tragus bent forward (Photo Wood)

Description: Upperparts brown to orange-brown, underparts brown. Flight membrane also brown, which gives a general colour of uniformly brown. Ears with long tragus, bent forward (Figure 3.129). The most distinctive characteristic that identifies this bat from all other insectivorous bats is the presence of only a single pair of upper incisors which are large and conical.

Measurements: (52 specimens), HB 60.0-75.0 mm, T 43.0-51.0 mm, FA 47.0-53.5 mm, Tb 17.0-20.0 mm, E 13.0-15.0 mm, Wt 17.0-25.0 g.

Echolocation: Frequency-modulated sweeps of average duration 7.4 ms, starting at 49 kHz and ending in a CF component with a peak frequency of 40 kHz and end frequency of 37 kHz (12 individuals, 286 calls, flying 5-10 m above ground) (T. Wood unpub. data).

Ecology: This bat is frequently found associated with human habitation. In KWR it was found in buildings at the field stations on the reserve edge. Highly gregarious, they can be seen roosting in large colonies in the roofs of houses, old abandoned buildings and in crowns of palm trees in gardens. They are also common in rubber plantations, roosting in the holes of old rubber trees. They are found in forested areas at all elevations roosting in small colonies in the tree holes of dead trees, but are not as common as in urban and suburban areas. In urban areas they frequent lamp-posts immediately after dark for insect prey.

Breeding: Fifteen of 26 females examined were found pregnant. July (4 specimens), August (2), September (1), and November (2). Six of these were found with suckling young in May (2) and June (4). Wong et al. (2002) reported twinning in this species in Peninsular Malaysia.

IUCN: LR (lc).

Distribution in KWR: Mist-netted at a roost in a building at Jenderak Selatan, and over rivers at Kuala Gandah and Kuala Lompat (T. Wood unpub. data). Also recorded at Kuala Lompat by Heller and Volleth (1989).

Distribution: Bangladesh, Pakistan to Taiwan, south to Sri Lanka, Myanmar, Cambodia, Peninsular Malaysia, Java, Bali, Nusa Tenggara (Indonesia), southeast to Philippines, and Aru Islands (Indonesia).

Family Molossidae - Free-tailed Bats

This family comprises three genera and four species in Peninsular Malaysia. All three genera are represented at KWR, and three species. The thickened tail projects from the end of the interfemoral membrane hence the description "free-tailed" bats. The muzzle projects well beyond the lower jaw and there is no noseleaf.

Mops mops (de Blainville)

Malayan Free-tailed Bat
Kelawar Lubang Kayu

Description: The fur is uniformly dark brown to chestnut-brown or orange, although the underparts of some individuals may be slightly paler (Figure 3.130). The ears are joined over the top of the head by a narrow flap of skin (Figure 3.131). The upper lip is wrinkled. It has four upper cheek teeth in the upper tooth row; the extra small anterior premolar of *Chaerephon* is absent. As for all molossids, the thick tail projects beyond the tail membrane (Figure 3.132).

FIGURE 3.130 *Mops mops* (Photo Kingston)

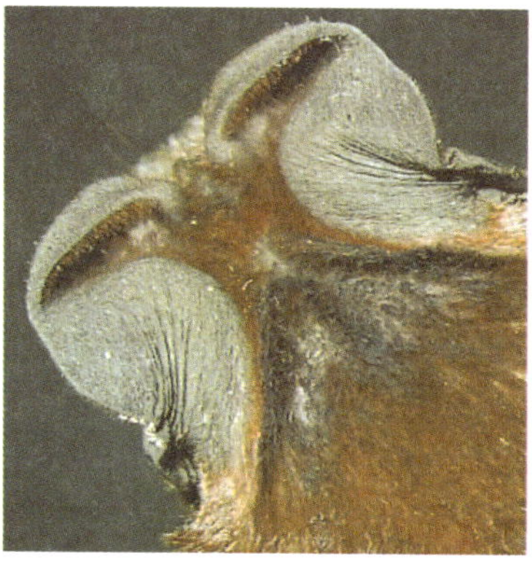

FIGURE 3.131 Dorsal view of narrow interaural band of skin connecting ears of *Mops mops* (Photo Wood)

Measurements: (11 specimens) HB 65.0-72.0 mm, T 35.0-39.0 mm, FA 40.0-45.0 mm, Tb 16.0-19.0 mm, E 18.0-22.0 mm, Wt 17.0-24.0 g. KWR: FA 41.0-43.9 mm, Wt 23.0-26.7 g (n = 4).

Echolocation: Alternating narrowband calls produced when flying > 10 m above ground. High-frequency calls start at a mean frequency of 37 kHz and end at c. 17 kHz, with mean peak frequency of 23 kHz and duration 15.5 ms. Low-frequency calls start at 26 kHz, end at 16 kHz with peak of 18.5 kHz and duration 16.7 ms (Kingston et al. 2003b).

FIGURE 3.132 Tail of *Mops mops* – typical of the Molossidae (Photo Kingston)

Ecology: Primarily a forest inhabitant, most easily captured foraging over rivers as it otherwise forages above the forest canopy or high in large clearings. It roosts in holes of dead and hollow trees. Often found roosting together with *Cheiromeles torquatus*.

Breeding: One of the five females examined was pregnant with a single embryo in January.

IUCN: LR(lc).

Distribution in KWR: Captured in mist nets set over the Lompat River at Kuala Lompat and Lubuk Baung, and the Teris River at Kuala Gandah (T. Wood unpub. data).

Distribution: Peninsular Malaysia, Sumatra, Borneo, and perhaps Java.

Chaerephon johorensis (Dobson)

Northern Free-tailed Bat
(Dato Meldrum's Bat)
Kelasar Johor

Description: Similar in colouration to *M. mops*, distinguished by having an enclosed pocket created by the interaural band of skin which is thick with a median ridge (Figures 3.133 and 3.134). A tuft of hairs on the underside of the interaural band is apparent when the band is everted. Unlike *M. mops* this species has five cheek teeth in the upper tooth row, including a small unicuspid anterior premolar.

FIGURE 3.133 *Chaerephon johorensis* with tuft of hairs from interaural band partially erected (Photo Wood)

Measurements: (19 specimens) HB 60.0-72.0 mm, T 36.0-43.0 mm, FA 44.0-48.0 mm, Tb 16.0-19.0 mm, E 16.0-22.0 mm, Wt 16.0-22.0 g.

Echolocation: Narrowband calls that alternate in peak frequency when the bat is flying higher than 10 m above the ground. High-frequency calls start at a mean frequency of 31 kHz and end at c. 17 kHz, with mean peak frequency of 21 kHz and duration 15.7 ms. Low-frequency calls start at 22 kHz, end at 14 kHz with peak of 17 kHz and duration 17.5 ms (Kingston et al. 2003b).

Ecology: Forages high above the canopy or in large gaps, and over large, slow rivers.

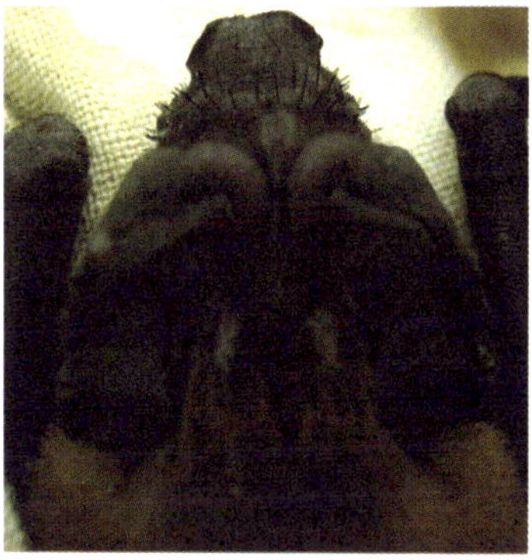

FIGURE 3.134 Dorsal view of thick interaural band of skin connecting ears of *Chaerephon johorensis* (Photo Wood)

Breeding: Of seven females examined, two were found pregnant with a single embryo each in June (1 specimen) and October (1).

IUCN: LR (nt).

Distribution in KWR: Captured in mist nets set of the Lompat River at Kuala Gandah and Kuala Lompat (T. Wood unpub. data); also recorded at Kuala Lompat (Kingston et al. 2003a).

Distribution: Peninsular Malaysia, and Sumatra.

Cheiromeles torquatus Horsfield

Greater Naked Bat
Kelawar Batin

FIGURE 3.135 *Cheiromeles torquatus* (Photo Kingston)

Description: This is the largest insectivorous bat in the Old World, and the largest aerial insectivore worldwide, weighing up to 200 g (Figure 3.135). The body is almost completely bald, with just a few short hairs on the underside, and a patch of hair in a shallow pocket under the neck (gular pouch) (Figure 3.136). Secretions from the gular pouch are extremely pungent. There are scattered hairs on the feet, and a stiff brush of short bristles on the first toe of the hind foot (Figure 3.137), presumably used in grooming. The head is very broad, with relatively small, rounded ears for a molossid that are not joined by any membrane, and the lips are smooth (Figure 3.135). The wings are extremely long and narrow, wingspan > 60 cm. When at rest, the tips of the wings are tucked away into subaxillary pouches created by a fold of skin that runs from the upper arm to the hip, opening to the rear (Figure 3.138). This enables the bat to move about quadrupedally, and can be

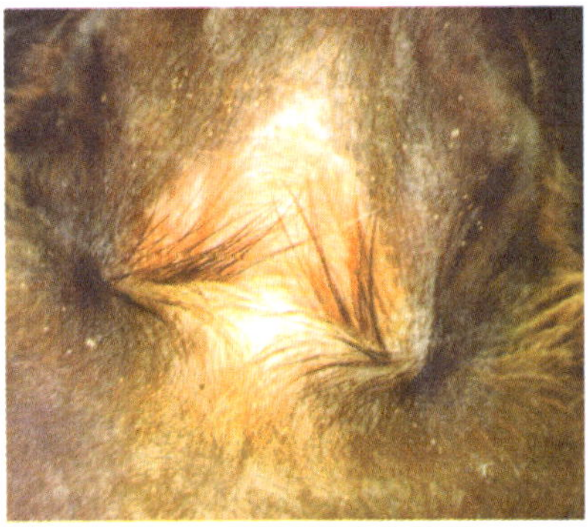

FIGURE 3.136 Gular pouch of *Cheiromeles torquatus* with hairs (Photo Kingston)

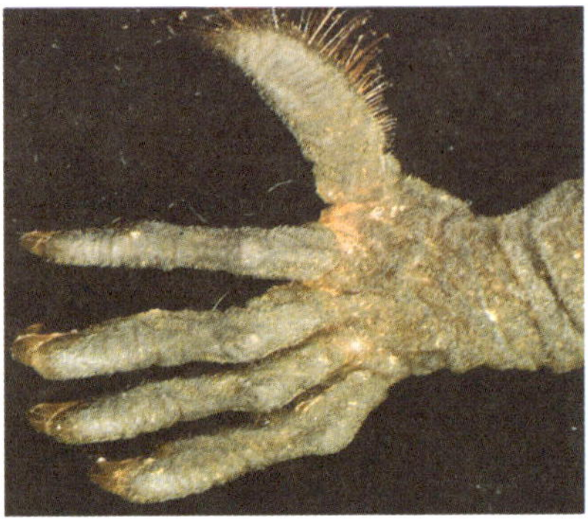

FIGURE 3.137 Hind foot of *Cheiromeles torquatus* to show stiff brush of bristles (Photo Kingston)

closed up with a muscular 'drawstring'. The hallux (the 'big toe') is set at right angles to the other digits of the hind foot (Figure 3.137), another adaptation to arboreal and terrestrial locomotion (Figure 139) (Schutt & Simmons 2001).

Measurements: (35 specimens) HB 125.0-180.0 mm, T 60.0-75.0 mm, FA 65-85 mm, Tb 35.0-43.0 mm, E 25.0-82.0 mm, Wt 115.0-180.0 g. KWR: FA 78.1-86.2 mm (n = 4), Wt 155.0-185.0 g (n = 3).

Echolocation: In search phase, *C. torquatus* alternates between calls that differ in frequency. High-frequency calls have a mean initial frequency of ca. 48 kHz, terminal frequency of ca. 25 kHz with peak frequency at ca. 29 kHz, and duration of 22 ms. In low-frequency calls mean initial frequency is 32 kHz, terminal frequency is 19 kHz, peak frequency is at 24 kHz and duration 21 ms (Kingston et al. 2003b). Heller (1995) also reported this alternation, but with peak frequencies at 28 kHz and 20 kHz.

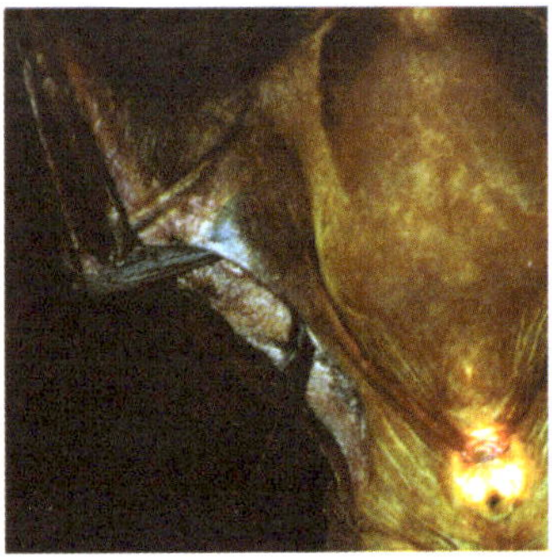

FIGURE 3.138 Ventral view of *Cheiromeles torquatus* showing wing tip folded in right subaxiallary pouch (Photo Kingston)

Ecology: Inhabits lowland to hill forest, and roosts in caves, old abandoned build-

FIGURE 3.139 *Cheiromeles torquatus* reversing up a tree (Photo Juliana)

FIGURE 3.140 Earwig on the hind limb of *Cheiromeles torquatus* (Photo Kingston)

ings, holes of large hollow trees. They are highly gregarious, roosting in large colonies, often in association with *Mops mops*. Lim (1973) found a colony roosting in a large hole of a dead tualang tree in Lake Temenggor, Upper Perak. An estimation of the population was made through waves of flight in the evening hours at 5 minutes interval, and indicated the presence of approximately 4,000 individuals. Feeds on large flying insects including large flying ants and termites. Typically forages high over the forest or clearings, and over rivers. They are able to swim to the banks should they fall in. Wing loading is the highest known for any bat at 39 Nm^{-2}, which in combination with an aspect ratio just under nine, suggests extremely fast, efficient flight. However, take-off is more difficult without a clear drop to gain lift. They appear unable to take off from the ground, and if grounded will walk to a vertical object (such as a tree), and reverse up it to gain height, and this may in part explain the extremely strong hind limbs, sharp claws and other terrestrial/arboreal adaptations. Large colonies of *Cheiromeles* are associated with a distinct earwig suborder (Arixenina), with 5 species included in 2 genera (Figure 3.140). They are wingless and almost blind, and while some species depend primarily on guano, others feed on skin debris and secretions of the animals themselves. They are found in the pouch as well as on the naked body. The ectoparasite is quite large, looking more like a cockroach than an earwig. It has a strong smell somewhat similar to cedar-wood oil.

Breeding: Of the 15 females examined, four were found to be pregnant with a single embryo each in June (1 specimen), August (1), September (1), and December (1).

Conservation Status: Numbers are declining throughout Malaysia. Despite the strong smell the bat is eaten by the Orang Asli and is a reserve food source for the community. Historically, the bat has been persecuted by farmers as a consequence of the false impression that it is a pest of rice crops. Niah Cave in Sarawak formerly supported an enormous colony of nearly 200,000 bats in the 1970s. Despite full legal protection in Sarawak, disturbance at the roost (primarily for collection of cave swiftlet nests), hunting of the bat itself, and loss of forest habitat around the cave had reduced numbers to 1,000 by 1992.

IUCN: LR (nt). The Species Action Plan for *C. torquatus* lists the following objectives: 1. Restore this unique species to its 1970 status; 2. Undertake further survey work and research to develop and implement a Recovery Plan that includes management of cave swiftlet populations (Hutson et al. 2001).

Distribution in KWR: Captured in mist nets set over the Lompat River at Kuala Lompat and Lubuk Baung, and Teris River at Kuala Gandah. Also recorded at Kuala Lompat by Kingston et al. (2003a).

Distribution: Peninsular Malaysia, Sumatra, Java, Borneo, and Palawan (Philippines).

References

Beck, A. and B. L. Lim, B. L. 1973. Reproductive biology of *Eonycteris spelaea*, Dobson (Megachiroptera) in West Malaysia. Acta Tropica 30: 251-260.

Campbell, P., C. J. Schneider, Adura M. Adnan, Zubaid Akbar and T. H. Kunz. 2004. Phylogeny and phylogeography of Old World fruit bats in the *Cynopterus brachyotis* complex. *Molecular Phylogenetics and Evolution* 33:764-781.

Chuen, W. W., D. Eaton and Y. M. Dan. 1998. Estimation of petai consumption in the Klang Valley in Peninsular Malaysia. In *Conservation, Management and Development of Forest Resources*, edited by S. S. Lee, Y. M. Dan, I. Gauld and J. Bishop. Proceedings of the Malaysia-United Kingdom Programme Workshop 21-24 October 1996. Malaysia: FRIM.

Chivers, D. J. 1980. *Malayan Forest Primates: Ten Years' Study in Tropical Rainforest.* New York: Plenum Press.

Corbet, G. B. and J. E. Hill. 1992. *The Mammals of the Indomalayan Region: A Systematic Review.* Oxford: Oxford University Press.

Findley, J. S. 1993. *Bats: A Community Perspective.* London: Cambridge University Press.

Francis, C. M. 1989. Notes on fruit bats (Chiroptera, Pteropodidae) from Malaysia and Brunei, with a description of a new subspecies of *Megaerops wetmorei* Taylor, 1934. *Canadian Journal of Zoology* 67: 2878-2882.

Francis, C. M. 1994. Vertical stratification of fruit bats (Pteropodidae) in lowland dipterocarp forest in Malaysia. *Journal of Tropical Ecology* 10: 523-530.

Francis, C. M., E. L. P. Anthony, J. A. Brunton and T. H. Kunz. 1994. Lactation in male fruit bats. *Nature* 367: 691-692.

Francis, C. M., T. Kingston and Zubaid Akbar (In prep. – *Acta Chiropterologica*). A new species of *Kerivoula* (Chiroptera: Vespertilionidae) from Peninsular Malaysia.

Fujita, M. S. and M. D. Tuttle, M. D. 1991. Flying foxes (Chiroptera: Pteropodidae): Threatened animals of key ecological and economic importance. *Conservation Biology* 5: 455-463.

Gould, E. 1978a. Foraging behaviour of Malaysian nectar-feeding bats. *Biotropica* 10:184-193.

Gould, E. 1978b. Opportunistic feeding by tropical bats. *Biotropica* 10:75-76.

Gould, E. 1978c. Rediscovery of *Hipposideros ridleyi* and seasonal reproduction in Malaysian bats. *Biotropica* 10: 30-32.

Heideman, P. D. and R. C. B. Utzurrum. 2003. Seasonality and synchrony of reproduction in three species of nectarivorous Philippines bats. *BMC Ecology* 3: 11.

Heller, K. –G. 1989. Echolocation calls of Malaysian bats. *Zeitschrift für Säugetierkunde* 54: 1-8.

Heller, K. –G. 1995. Echolocation and body size in insectivorous bats: the case of the giant naked bat *Cheiromeles torquatus* (Molossidae). *Le Rhinolophe* 11:27-38.

Heller, K. –G. and M. Volleth. 1989. Fledermäuse aus Malaysia. I. Beobachtungen zur Biologie, Morphologie und Taxonomie. *Senckenbergiana Biologica* 69:243-276.

Heller, K. –G., R. Achmann and K. Witt. 1993. Monogamy in the bat *Rhinolophus sedulus*? *Zeitschrift für Säugetierkunde* 58: 376-377.

Hodgkison, R. 2001. The ecology of fruit bats (Chiroptera: Pteropodidae) in a Malaysian lowland dipterocarp forest, with particular reference to the spotted-winged fruit bat (*Balionycteris maculata*, Thomas). Ph.D. Diss., University of Aberdeen.

Hodgkison, R., S. T. Balding, Zubaid Akbar and T. H. Kunz. 2003a. Fruit bats (Chiroptera: Pteropodidae) as seed dispersers and pollinators in a lowland Malaysian rainforest. *Biotropica* 35: 491-502.

Hodgkison, R., S. T. Balding, Zubaid Akbar and T. H. Kunz. 2003b. Roosting ecology and social organization of the spotted-winged fruit bat, *Balionycteris maculata* (Chiroptera: Pteropodidae), in a Malaysian lowland dipterocarp forest. *Journal of Tropical Ecology* 19: 667-676.

Hodgkison, R., S. T. Balding, Zubaid Akbar and T. H. Kunz. 2004a. Habitat structure, wing morphology, and the vertical stratification of Malaysian fruit bats (Megachiroptera: Pteropodidae). *Journal of Tropical Ecology* 20: 667-673.

Hodgkison, R., S. T. Balding, Zubaid Akbar and T. H. Kunz. 2004b. Temporal variation in the relative abundance of fruit bats (Megachiroptera: Pteropodidae) in relation to the availability of food in a lowland Malaysian rainforest. *Biotropica* 36: 522-533.

Hutson, A. M., S. P. Mickleburgh and P. A. Racey, (comp.) 2001. *Microchiropteran bats: Global status survey and conservation action plan.* Gland, Switzerland and Cambridge, UK: IUCN/SSC Chiroptera Specialist Group, IUCN.

Juliana Senawi. 2004. Spatial variation in diversity parameters of insectivorous bat assemblages at Krau, Malaysia. Master's Thesis. Universiti Kebangsaan Malaysia, Bangi, Selangor D. E.

Kick, S. A. 1982. Target detection by the echolocating bat *Eptesicus fuscus. Journal of Comparative Physiology* 145: 431-435.

Kingston, T., T. H. Kunz, R. Hodgkison and Zubaid Akbar. 1997. *Phoniscus jagorii,* a vespertilionid bat newly recorded from Peninsular Malaysia. *Malayan Nature Journal* 50: 363.

Kingston, T., G. Jones, Zubaid Akbar and T. H. Kunz. 1999. Echolocation signal design in Kerivoulinae and Murininae (Chiroptera: Vespertilionidae) from Malaysia. *Journal of Zoology* 249: 359-374.

Kingston, T., G. Jones, Zubaid Akbar and T. H. Kunz 2000a. Resource partitioning in rhinolophoid bats revisited. *Oecologia* 124: 332-342.

Kingston, T., G. Jones, Zubaid Akbar and T. H. Kunz 2000b. Social calls in clear-winged woolly bats (*Kerivoula pellucida*) from Malaysia. *Bioacoustics* 11: 1-16.

Kingston, T., M. Lara, G. Jones, Zubaid Akbar, T. H. Kunz and C. J. Schneider. 2001. Acoustic divergence in two cryptic *Hipposideros* species: A role for social selection? *Proceedings of the Royal Society of London, Series B* 268: 1381-1386.

Kingston, T., C. M. Francis, Zubaid Akbar, T. H. Kunz. 2003a. Species richness in an insectivorous bat assemblage from Malaysia. *Journal of Tropical Ecology* 19: 67-79.

Kingston, T., C. M. Francis, Zubaid Akbar, T. H. Kunz. 2003b. Alternation of echolocation calls in five species of aerial-feeding insectivorous bats from Malaysia. *Journal of Mammalogy* 84: 205-215.

Kingston, T. et al. (in press). The Malaysian Bat Conservation Research Unit: Research, capacity building and education in an Old World hotspot. In *Proceedings of the National Seminar On Protected Areas.* Universiti Kebangsaan Malaysia.

Kofron, C. P. 1994. Bamboo-roosting of the thick-thumbed pipistrelle bat (*Glischropus tylopus*) in Borneo. *Mammalia* 58: 306-309.

Lekagul, B. and J. A. McNeely. 1988. *Mammals of Thailand.* 2nd Edition. Bangkok: Darnsutha Press.

Lim, B. L. 1967. Abundance and distribution of Malaysian bats in different ecological habitats. *Federation Museum Journal (N.S.)* 152: 375-379.

Lim, B. L. 1970. Food habits and breeding cycle of the Malaysian fruit-eating bat, *Cynopterus brachyotis*. *Journal of Mammalogy* 51: 174-177

Lim, B. L. 1973. Breeding pattern, food habits, and parasitic infection of bats in Gunung Brinchang. *Malayan Nature Journal* 26: 6-13.

Marshall, A. G. 1971. The ecology of *Basilia hispida* (Diptera: Nycteribiidae) in Malaysia. *Journal of Animal Ecology* 40: 141-154.

Marshall, A. G. 1980. The comparative ecology of insects ectoparasitic upon bats in West Malaysia. In *Proceedings of the Fifth International Bat Research Conference*, edited by D. E. Wilson and A. L. Gardner. Lubbock, Texas: Texas Tech. Press.

Marshall, A. G. 1982. The ecology of the bat ectoparasite *Eoctenes spasmae* (Hemiptera: Polyctenidae) in Malaysia. *Biotropica* 14: 50-55.

Marshall, A. G. 1985. Old World phytophagous bats (Megachiroptera) and their food plants: A survey. *Zoological Journal of the Linnean Society* 83: 351-369.

Medway, Lord. 1972. Reproductive cycles of flat-headed bats *Tylonycteris pachypus* and *T. robustula* (Chiroptera: Vespertilioninae) in a humid equatorial environment. *Zoological Journal of the Linnean Society, London* 51:33-61

Medway, Lord. 1972. The Gunong Benom expedition 1967. 6. The distribution and altitudinal zonation of birds and mammals on Gunong Benom. *Bulletin of the British Museum (Natural History) Zoology* 23:105-116.

Medway, Lord. 1983. *The wild mammals of Malaya (Peninsular Malaysia) and Singapore*. 2nd Edition, revised. Kuala Lumpur: Oxford University Press.

Medway, Lord and D. R. Wells. 1971. Diversity and density of birds and mammals at Kuala Lompat, Pahang. *Malayan Nature Journal* 24: 238-247.

Medway, Lord and A. G. Marshall. 1972. Roosting associations of flat-headed bats, *Tylonycteris* species (Chiroptera: Vespertilionidae) in Malaysia. *Journal of Zoology* 168: 463-482.

Mickleburgh, S., A. Hutson, and P. A. Racey (comp.) 1992. *Old World Fruit Bats: An action plan for their conservation.* Gland, Switzerland and Cambridge, UK: IUCN/SSC Chiroptera Specialist Group, IUCN.

Myers, N. 1985. *The primary source: Tropical forests and our future.* New York and London: Norton.

Neuweiler, G. 1990. Auditory adaptations for prey capture in echolocating bats. *Physiological Review* 79: 615-641.

Neuweiler, G. and M. B. Fenton. 1988. Behavior and foraging ecology of echolocating bats. In *Animal sonar: Processes and performance*, edited by P. E. Natchigall and P. W. B. Moore 535-549. New York: Plenum Press.

Norberg, U. M. and J. M. V. Rayner. 1987. Ecological morphology and flight in bats: Wing adaptations, flight performance, foraging strategy and echolocation. *Philosophical Transactions of the Royal Society of London B* 316: 335-427.

Novick, A. 1958. Orientation in Paleoptropical bats. 2. Megachiroptera. *Journal of Experimental Zoology* 137: 443-461.

Pavey, C. R. and C. J. Burwell. 1997. The diet of the diadem leaf-nosed bat *Hipposideros diadema*: Confirmation of a morphologically-based prediction of carnivory. *Journal of Zoology* 243: 295-303.

Payne, J. and C. M. Francis. 1985. *A Field Guide to the Mammals of Borneo.* Kuala Lumpur: The Sabah Society and World Wildlife Fund.

Shilton, L.A., J. D. Altringham, S. G. Compton, and R. J. Whittaker. 1999. Old World fruit bats can be long-distance seed dispersers through extended retention of viable seeds in the gut. *Proceedings of the Royal Society of London Series B.* 266: 219-223.

Schnitzler, H.-U and K. M. V. Kalko. 1998. How echolocating bats search and find food. In *Bat biology and conservation*, edited by T. H. Kunz and P. A. Racey, 193-196. Washington, D.C: Smithsonian Institution Press.

Schulz, M. 2000. Roosts used by the golden-tipped bat, *Kerivoula papuensis* (Chiroptera: Vespertilionidae). *Journal of Zoology (London)* 250:467-478.

Schutt, W. A. and N. B. Simmons. 2001. Morphological specializations of *Cheiromeles* (naked bulldog bats; Molossidae) and their possible role in quadrupedal locomotion. *Acta Chiropterologica* 3: 225-235.

Simmons, N. B. In Press. *Chiroptera.* In *Mammal Species of the World: A Taxonomic and Geographic Reference,* edited by D. E. Wilson, D.E. and D. M. Reeder. 3rd Edition. Washington: Smithsonian Institution Press.

Start, A. 1974. The feeding biology in relation to food resources of nectarivorous bats (Chiroptera: Macroglossinae) in Malaysia. Ph.D. Diss., University of Aberdeen.

Start, A. and A. G. Marshall. 1975. Nectarivorous bats as pollinators of trees in West Malaysia. In *Tropical trees: Variation, breeding and conservation*, edited by J. Burley and B. T. Styles 141-150. London: Academic Press.

Surlykke, A., L. A. Miller, B. Mohl, B. B. Andersen, J. Christensendalsgaard, and M. B. Jorgensen 1993. Echolocation in two very small bats from Thailand – *Craseonycteris thonglongyai* and *Myotis siligorensis. Behavioral Ecology and Sociobiology* 33: 1-12.

Tan, K. H., A. Zubaid and T. H. Kunz. 1997. Tent construction and social organization in *Cynopterus brachyotis* (Muller) (Chiroptera: Pteropodidae) in Peninsular Malaysia. *Journal of Natural History* 31: 1605-1621.

Tan, K. H., A. Zubaid and T. H. Kunz. 1998. Food habits of *Cynopterus brachyotis* (Muller) (Chiroptera: Pteropodidae) in Peninsular Malaysia. *Journal of Tropical Ecology* 14: 299-307.

Tan, K. H., A. Zubaid and T. H. Kunz. 1999. Roost selection and social organization in *Cynopterus horsfieldii* (Chiroptera: Pteropodidae). *Malayan Nature Journal* 53: 105-110.

Wong, C. H., Y. L. Gee, A. Zubaid and A. B. Kamis. 2002. Twinning in *Scotophilus kuhlii* (Microchiroptera: Vespertilionidae) from Peninsular Malaysia. *Malaysian applied Biology* 31: 71-73.

Zhang, S. Y, H. H. Zhao, J. Feng, L. X. Sheng, H. Wang and L. X. Wang, L. 2000. Relationship between echolocation frequency and body size in two species of hipposiderid bats. *Chinese Science Bulletin* 45: 1587-1590

Zubaid, A. 1988. Food habits of *Hipposideros armiger* (Chiroptera, Rhinolophidae) from Peninsular Malaysia. *Mammalia* 52: 585-588.

Zubaid, A. 1990. Food and roosting habits of the black-bearded tomb bat, *Taphozous melanopogon* (Chiroptera, Emballonuridae) from Peninsular Malaysia. *Mammalia* 54: 159-162.

Zubaid, A. 1993. A comparison of the bat fauna between a primary and fragmented secondary forest in Peninsular Malaysia. *Mammalia* 57: 201-206.

Index